# Contents


| | |
|---|---|
| Preface | 9 |
| Kilbirnie—an introduction | 13 |
| Reading, writing, 'rithmetic | 16 |
| Picture gallery of Kilbirnie —Past and present | 31 |
| Pastimes | 55 |
| Industry and shops | 64 |
| Churches of Kilbirnie | 82 |
| Clubs and Societies | 88 |
| Transport | 99 |
| Decades of Change | 101 |
| Monuments and Buildings | 105 |
| Retrospective | 113 |
| Events | 119 |

# Kilbirnie
# &
# Glengarnock

## Shared Memories

# Kilbirnie
# &
# Glengarnock
## Shared Memories

*compiled by*

**Moira Kinniburgh**
&
**Fiona Burke**

Library Services

**Kilbirnie Library**
**1995**

Cunninghame District Council
Leisure Services

ISBN No 1 897998 01 5

*Printed by*
Cordfall Ltd
0141 332 4640

## HOUSE OF COMMONS

### LONDON SW1A 0AA

Kilbirnie is a community of great character and integrity, supported by a wealth of history. Industrial closures of recent years have dealt it many blows, but the resilience of its people continues to shine through. I am proud to represent Kilbirnie at Parliamentary level.

This valuable book explores many aspects of Kilbirnie's history, both ancient and modern; spiritual and industrial. Everyone who lives in the town or has an affection for it will gain fresh awareness of the forces which have created Kilbirnie as it is today. The challenge now is to ensure its successful future.

BRIAN WILSON<br>MP for Cunninghame North

# Preface

About two and a half years ago, fuelled by enthusiasm, we decided to attempt to collate some of the history of Kilbirnie into a publication. Initially, we had a very well attended open evening featuring old historical photos, two Kilbirnie people to talk, and our local history librarian who outlined the need to preserve historical detail. After that, many people, residents and former residents, began to lend us treasured photos and mementoes and a committee was formed to collate the information. The committee consisted of Moira Kinniburgh, Fiona Burke, Judith Davenport, Jean McCulloch, Pat Sloss, Joseph McTaggart, Agnes Harris and Hugh Law. All helped enormously with their input of ideas, articles and photos. These were itemised and stored in a safe place in the library and since we had the only access to them, the natural progression was for us to continue with the publication using this material.

Everyone has been patient while waiting for this publication. We did not realise what a momentous but most enjoyable task we had taken on and have merely scratched at the surface in this volume. Perhaps someone will take on the mantle to document more of Kilbirnie's history in the future, our time being limited to library hours.

We are indebted to the many people who entrusted us with sentimental and irreplaceable photography and memorabilia and say a hearty thank you to them all, and to Alasdair MacNaughtan, Library Services Manager who encouraged and supported our idea.

Thanks to our committee and to Mr Fyfe, Mr Duncan, Mrs Piper and Mrs McConnell who let us visit their homes to tape record their memories and to Irene Caldwell who later transcribed them and did much of our typing—not an easy task given some of our scribblings! Hugh Law, Mrs Williamson, Mrs Fitzsimmons, Ian Johnstone, Jack Gibson, Jim Duffield, Jim Hunter, Monica Tipping, Mr Taylor, Mr Miller, Wallace Jones, John King amongst others all took time to write articles and anecdotes for us and supported us throughout. Gale McLeod started working in the library and ended up deciphering more of our notes and converting them all into neat manuscript form. Thanks to David Martin who answered many phone calls from us and to Jill McColl our present local history librarian who read the rough manuscript. Brian Wilson took time from his House of Commons duties to write our foreword. Thanks to Carol his PA who kept him informed of our progress.

Lastly we would like to say how much we've enjoyed working on this, how glad we are that we've got to this stage and, that we hope you all enjoy our look at Kilbirnie. Perhaps others will follow from other pens. We hope we have all the facts correct but you know where to find us! Meanwhile champagne at last!

Moira Kinniburgh
Fiona Burke,
Kilbirnie Library.

## The Co Nock *Sanny Tod*

It's money a lang and weary day
Since the year 1889
When I came tae Kilbirnie toon
Tae let folk's see the time

There's lots o' things that I has seen
Keep mind I'm tellin' ye
Especially on a Saturday night
An' it's no' wi' drinkin' tea

The Institute that stauns ower there
Was gifted for your pleasure
And people came from far and near
Tae spend an hour o' leisure

The Robert William Knox Memorial
With its bright burning light
Is there for ane an' a' tae see
And guide ye hame at night

The Brig itself has changed a bit
It's been made fairly wide
Tae suit the enormous traffic
For Largs and West Kilbride

The thacked hoose across the Brig
Lang sine's been torn doon
And a mission hall's been built
For the guid folk o' the toon

A Picture House and Cafe
Is where auld Low's Mansion stood
For tae entertain the folk
When they are in the mood

Forbye the numerous changes
That hae taken place
I've seen auld ane's slip awa
That weel a kent their faces

On racing days I watch the punters
Luk up tae see the time
Before makin' for the bookie
Tae pit on their wee bit line

And then there is ither folk
Always in a fuss
Hurriedly they glance at me
When gaun tae catch a bus

Last winter some bad boys
Plastered me with snaw
Stoppin' me hands frae gaun roon
And I lost an hour or twa

Many pleasant memories I have
Of Byegone days spent here
Watching the happy crowds
Bringing in New Year

When I look down on tae the road
Where the Pub and Smiddy used
tae staun
I ken my days are drawing near
And that might no' be long

Noo when that time comes
And they decide tae scrap the Auld
Co' Nock
Remember me when I'm awa'
Guidbye Kilbirnie folk.

## The Co Nock *Elizabeth J Steele*

A came to the toon in eighty nine
Sae proud an fair o' face
But a hunner year on they took me
doon
A doot am in disgrace

A thought a'd served the toon folk
weel
But it only goes tae show
That whether they need yer face or
yer hons
When its yur turn ye've got tae go

The day they decided ma time and
fate
Maist folk were on the dole
The Co was knocked doon in eighty
eight
And ma place wis jist a hole

That hole had been filled fur ninety
nine years
Though changes had tane place
o'aroon
Bit never before had ony yin dared
Suggest taking the Co Nock doon

Although I'm lying low the noo
Wi thochts o'Auld Lang Syne
They say ma fate's tae change quite
soon
In NINETEEN eighty nine

That's the year ma place gets filled
Or so the Cooncil say
With hooses and offices trimmed wi
gilt
By that will be some day

The planners though were awfy
long
The builders awfy slow
If ma hons moved as slow as theirs
A wid've been shifted long ago

When the time wis by for lyin low
A wis lifted fae ma tomb
Ma face cleaned up and luking
braw
They wur gein me back ma room

They say disappointment hits ye
hard
They nearly broke ma heart
When looking out this fancy case
A nearly did'ny start.

Ma view had gone a could'ny see
Across ma maybole brig
Where many an hour a passed ma
time
Wi folk in song and jig

Its no the same am sad tae say
A'll ne're get o'ver the shock
No only did they change ma place
"I AM NOW THE COUNCIL
CLOCK"

A'll tick away for madern times
But when a come tae stop
Lay me tae rest wi words that say
"Here lies the Old Co Nock"

# Kilbirnie—an introduction

Kilbirnie is a small town in the West of Scotland situated about 20 miles south of Glasgow and has a population of 8,194. (Jan 1993)

It was originally a parish of farms with a community centre at the Kirk but, unlike other towns, it did not grow up round the church but around its Mill Industry followed by the Steel Industry.

The name Kilbirnie may be derived from the Celtic "Kil" meaning Church and "Birnie" or "Birnus" from the church dedicated to St. Birnie. This seems the most logical derivation but it could also have been named after St. Brendan, a Gaelic speaking Missionary who lived about 150 years before St. Birnie. There was a yearly celebration called Brinan's Day which was held on the anniversary of St. Brendan and there was also a well called St. Birnie's Well.

The Auld Kirk has been the subject of many excursions to Kilbirnie throughout its history and there have been numerous newspaper articles and diaries relating to these excursions.

In Roman times a Crannog or Artificial Island was built on Kilbirnie Loch. They were quite common in Scotland but it was not discovered until later that there had been canoe people inhabiting this island. It had been thought it was a bird sanctuary.

The small community of farms and tenants on the local estates were encouraged by the lairds to set themselves up as traders. Many of the farms are long gone but their names live on in streets called after them: Sersley, Dennyholm, Craighouse, Holmhead (Holms Farm).

Kilbirnie has quite a few well known links through history, not the least of them, Thomas Crawfurd who stormed the Castle in Dumbarton causing irreparable damage to Mary Queen of Scots' army and directly linked with her downfall. He had been Darnley's gentleman and of course,

*The Cross and Main Street, Kilbirnie*

opposed Mary. However, the Poet Laird of Ladyland was one of Mary Queen of Scots supporters and lost his life trying to garrison Ailsa Craig for her.

In 1707, strangely enough the year of the Crown Union between Scotland and England, the baronies of Kilbirnie and Glengarnock were ratified under the Great Seal of the Lands. After this, Kilbirnie started to thrive and in 1788, Knox's Mill opened and the town grew up around it and the other mills.

In 1845, Merry and Cunninghame erected 8 Blast Furnaces for the production of pig iron using local black band coal and ironstone. The pig iron was sold under the trade name of "Glengarnock" and there was a large trade with America. When the Americans developed their own industry, trade was reduced so steel making processes were introduced.

The first cast of steel was made in June 1885. In 1890, Merry and Cunninghame's interests in the plant were dissolved and the Glengarnock Iron and Steel company was formed. In 1916, this was in turn purchased by David Colville and Sons Limited. They had rented the premises from 1915 as required to produce munitions of war. In 1930, Colville and Sons amalgamated with James Dunlop and Company and formed Colville's

***Houston Painting. Now in Kilbirnie Library***

Limited. There was a Public House situated within the perimeter of the Steelworks called Billy Ruffins and the Lithuanian refugees who were employed in the Steelworks and lived in the Raws were known to buy a pail of beer. The Steelworks operated albeit with dwindling work and staff until 1985 when it finally closed down—a very depressing time.

In 1867 the Garnock Burns Club was established and at one Burns Supper in early 1900, one of the toasts very much reflected the industry of the town.

Here's tae auld Kilbirnie toon
O toons roon here it taks the lead
Here's tae the ropes, chairs, Herrin nets,
Glengarnock Steel and Knox's threads.

The Burns Club still exists at present.

A very grand affair was the opening of Knox's Institute in 1892 which the papers covered in great detail with the local paper listing all the participants.

Kilbirnie Library at the moment is home to a painting by Robert Houston, one of a well known family in the town. At the 1910 Ideal Home Exhibition, James Houston of Craighouse won a bronze medal in the trade section and Robert Houston, Glenlogan, won a silver medal for a landscape in oils.

After World War I, housing schemes began to spring up in Britain reaching Kilbirnie after the 20s. Glenriddet was built between the wars and the new Longbar was built in 1935 re-housing people from the old houses at the "Longbar", the "Raws" at the Steelworks and the "Den" between Kilbirnie and Dalry. After the War came the Prefabs. Then in 1949, the Milton was built followed by the Fudstone in 1956. Later estates were built, such as, Herriot Avenue, Castle Grove and Dennyholm Wynd in 1993.

Kilbirnie like many other towns has had good times and bad and had to survive mass unemployment after the closing of the Steelworks—one of the biggest industries. But, it has survived. The people who were born there or live or even just visit, enjoy being part of the community. This is reflected in the many requests that have been made for a publication about Kilbirnie, Glengarnock, Longbar and has resulted in us undertaking this project to try to record a little of Kilbirnie's history.

# Reading, writing, 'rithmetic

Standards of education and indeed methods of teaching have changed over the period of time this publication covers, and are still changing. Education is compulsory and whether it was learning to write on a slate, use an ink well, or work on computer terminals, children attend school from the age of 5 where it is hoped they will at least learn the three R's.

Although some children don't like school or some aspect of school life, most would, in retrospect, recall some happy days and interesting stories.

*Grey School 1863—1992*

## GLENGARNOCK PRIMARY SCHOOL

Originally schooling was carried out in wooden huts near the "Caley Railway line". In 1863 there were 230 on the roll with James Baird as head.

In 1877, Robert Grey began as headmaster (why it was called 'Grey' School) with a roll of 400 with each pupil paying 6/6 (32p), fees yearly. In 1887 the bottom storey of Glengarnock School was built easing accommodation problems, with upstairs being added in 1903.

In 1910, Glengarnock won the junior schools football tournament. Also around this time free breakfasts and dinners were available to children as the resulting depression in trade and the miners' strike caused a reduction in income.

In 1921 New Central School opened and supplementary classes were transferred and in 1923 the 5 lowest infant classes were moved to new wooden accommodation on the other side of the River Garnock. The attendance was greatly influenced by the weather—when the Garnock rose, the school was closed as on 27th May 1925 when the infant department flooded.

From 1930 the school was modernised and in 1936, Mr D.B. McLean took over as head teacher.

*Central School, Kilbirnie*

IQ tests were given in school and the school dentist and doctor visited regularly. In the 1940s Air Raid Drill was carried out in the school, and in 1945 snowstorms closed the school for a few days. Free dinners were given around this time and a new dining hall was opened in 1947. In 1949 the school produced its first magazine.

When the Milton Scheme was built, the shift in population caused the school roll to fall. In 1953 one of the teachers, Miss Riddet, retired after 44 years service with no absences! She was followed a year later by the retirement of Mr McLean.

Latterly, Central School was used for the

beginners, primaries 1-3 and Glengarnock for primaries 4-7 which did not make administration easy.

Both schools closed in 1992 and the new Glengarnock Primary opened in Grahamston Avenue. Unfortunately, Central School and Glengarnock School buildings were demolished in late 1992 and at present (April 1993) are vacant sites. April 1994 saw the opening of the new Health Centre on the Central School site.

The earliest age for leaving school was at the age of 10 in 1870 and in those days the highest age was 14 with the cleverest children becoming pupil/teachers. Education now can continue at school until 6th year with opportunities for continuing at evening classes, colleges or universities. In the 1870s counting would be done using an abacus and punishments included one of the cane or the strap. Nowadays computers are widely used and the strap is nonexistent. Things were very demanding according to the early records of 1860-1870; the emphasis was very much on learning with very little relaxation and the teachers' work was inspected by the headmasters who would take lessons and reprimand or even dismiss a teacher whose class was found to be backward.

When I went to school as a five year old the Headmaster was Mr William Law, never known other than Bunny Law. I was newly started school when "The Wee School" was built and the infants were taken across the burn to it. This happened in 1923. This burn, the River Garnock, played quite a part in school life. On the road home from school, and sometimes on the way there, the great temptation was to play "doon the burn". Then there was the excitement when the burn was flooded. Parents from the village would come to collect their children and take them safely home, and those of us who went in the other direction felt somewhat cheated out of a few hours holiday. But the excitement was there just the same.

In those days, the playground was divided into a boys' section and a girls' section. In the boys' playground, football and "bools" were played in their own seasons and the girls engaged in "peever beds" and skipping. The classrooms were stepped up from the front, nearest to the teacher and the blackboard to the back where the brainy ones sat and of course, the boys on one half of the room and the girls had the other. The desks and seats were bolted to the floor and so could not be shuffled about, but the clatter of slates being put in their slots made just about as much noise. It was not easy to present your written sums, spelling etc., in a tidy manner unless you kept your slate pencil sharpened which you did by rubbing it against a wall or a stone. I am afraid hygiene was not high on our agenda! Once a week you did your written work in ink. How you hoped for a pen with a nib that did not scratch! It was so easy to have blots on your work, especially if your

*Demise of Glengarnock School*

*Glengarnock Primary School Circa 1950.*

*Beith and Glengarnock Staff at West Linton Camp School (D C McLean)*

*Hut Class 1937*

*P7 School Trip 1972. Flight around Ayrshire.*

The names of those who obtained Certificates for attendance are :-

| | | | |
|---|---|---|---|
| Jessie Richmond, | Parkhill, | Kilbirnie | (97·7%) |
| Daniel McKee, | 22 Milton Rd | do. | (97·6) |
| Jeanie Thomson (b). | Avonhaugh | do | (do) |
| Wm Calderwood, | 38 Hill St, | Glengarnock | (97·5) |
| James Reid, | 5 Cochrane St, | Kilbirnie | (97·0) |
| Wm Law, | 27 Muirend St | do. | (96·8) |
| Geo. Stevenson, | 44 Knoxville Rd | do. | (do) |
| Minnie Barclay, | 31 Schoolwynd | do | (96·6) |
| Annie Allan, | 8 Mill Rd | do | (96·4) |
| Mary Reid, | Reidhurst | do | (96·1) |
| Hugh Hamilton, | 28 Schoolwynd | do | (96·0) |
| Agnes Fraser, | 16 Muirend St | do | (do) |
| Robt Kane, | 7 Newton St | do. | (95·9) |
| Bessie Logan, | Masonic Temple | do | (do) |
| Kate Cochrane, | 22 Muirend St | do | (do) |
| Jeanie Thomson (a) | 14 Knoxville Rd | do | (95·7) |
| Agnes Johnston, | 16 Holmheads | do. | (95·4) |
| Wm Fyfe, | 39 do | do | (do) |
| May Whyte, | Glenholm, | Glengarnock | (95·3) |
| Archd McLeod, | 3 Parkend, | Kilbirnie | (95·2) |

*Central School*

inkwell had been newly filled. Handwriting was perfected by the use of a "Times copy book" where you traced over the letters and words before writing them freehand, all this was done in ink and so there was no second chance.

Many of the teachers were there for a lifetime and so became legends. My earliest recollections are of Miss Howie and Miss Gibson, but these are very faint ones. I have pleasant memories of many others. There was Miss Jean Dick who went as Infant Mistress to Bridgend School and became Mrs Henderson. Miss Mowatt was a gentle person whom we all loved, Miss May Jamieson I held in respect and was not too sure of.

Miss Jessie Anderson was a very ladylike person and Miss Jenny Kerr in the qualifying class was something of a character. Her memory was not too good and sometimes she forgot why she had sent you to stand on the floor for punishment and wanted to know why you were there! Many are the tales told about her, how many are true we can only guess! Miss Agnes Riddet was another teacher who served the children for a lifetime. I can also remember Miss Cochrane, Miss Muir, Miss Stewart and Miss Kirk somewhere along the line. Once a week we had "Drill" in the hall. A drill teacher named Miss Smith came for this. We stood in lines and did physical jerks. The smallest were at the front of the lines and it graduated to the tallest at the back. How glad I was to be at the back of the line as I was somewhat afraid of Miss Smith. I must have been something of a "stiffy"! Younger people will have their own memories of other teachers who came later, but these are the stalwarts of my childhood.

Life in the new school will be entirely different to what we remembered from our younger days. I wonder just how memories of it will differ from those of us "oldies". Maybe someone will be writing nostalgic memories of it in another hundred years. I can only guess!

## FEMALE INDUSTRIAL SCHOOL—1871

This school, also known as the Lady School, belonged to the Barony Church. Lessons were held in the church hall (now the Young Persons Institute) and were taught by female teachers only.

Some of the pupils attended school in the morning and worked in the mill in the afternoon—Half Timers.

Subjects were Geography, Arithmetic, Grammar, Spelling, Reading, Writing and History. Pupils ranged from 5 to 14 years and were charged weekly fees. The earliest records (1871) show there were 56 pupils and 2 teachers, Catherine Thomson and Agnes McDonald.

In 1893, the Roman Catholic pupils left to go to their new school and in 1915 the 2 highest classes were sent to Ladyland, resulting in the school roll numbers falling. In 1920 it was decided to close the school and pupils and teacher, Miss Turnbull, were instructed to report to Bridgend.

*Bridgend School*

## BRIDGEND—1893

Bridgend School was known to many as "Ballantyne's School" since Mr Ballantyne was the headmaster around 1900. The school roll was then divided into infants, juniors and seniors. The school received glowing reports from all who inspected it. In 1905, senior pupils were sent to Ladyland and by 1911 when Mr Law took over as head, the roll had risen to 368.

During the War, Mr Law assumed duties as head at Ladyland, as Mr Smith (head) was on army duty and attendance at the school was low due to poverty and disease. The roll dropped to 280 and in 1921 Mr Law moved to Glengarnock School and Bridgend joined with Ladyland School.

## 5 TO 14 IN THE TWENTIES

School days are happy days, so they say, but it all depends on how you look at them. Our memories start at Bridgend School (now the Community Centre), which we entered or were dragged into by fond mothers at 5. The school was like a little prison where you could not do as you liked.

Each one had a turn at the counting frame (the abacus), watched by Miss Smith (Kep a gush they called her—Guess why?), or Miss Armour with her nasal toned voice. In due course off to Ladyland School we went—big boys and girls now—to meet even bigger pupils. The headmaster with a big moustache was Jim Smith (known as Darkie). The teachers too were different and more scary with a big belt—you daren't move or speak. There was Miss Gracie in the "Quali" who loved to lead you from the back of the room to the front by your hair. There was no respect of persons with her and no favourites. Next door was Miss Isa Anderson with her golden hair and her favourite green dress. Miss Dick (Jenny), was small but a terror. Strap happy she was and would use her belt, then pull it through a piece of white paper to show how dirty your hand was. Miss Boyd was tall and stately but she meant business. At home time we would cross the "bundy burn" and down the "gum". It was a must to look in (no further), at Dolly Mack's shop [just demolished]. Many tales were told about this store. Down the Dennyholm we would go to visit Clark's Smiddy and catch the strong smell as Hugh Stirling made and put new shoes on a horse. Up the "Golden Stairs", we went not forgetting to look at Katy Cochrane's shop [now G Sneddon's] Past the Jubilee [now gone] then the Industrial School [now Y.P.I.], on to the "Glowering Lawn" and St. Bridget's School with Frank McIntyre in charge. Then came Paterson's Chip Shop positioned where the Library now stands. Down the hill and visit the Cottage Cafe belonging to Carlo Bernardo. He bred spaniels and a collection of hard bread was worth a "Pokey Hat".

Schooling reached its height at the Central School. The "Heidy" was Richard Liptrot (Lippy they called him—maybe because his belt was nippy!). His efficient staff included Annie Muir, Johnny Gibb and Rab Barclay (The "Jani"). The highlight of the school was in the early part of 1928 when Sir Charles Ferguson visited the school to present a flag sent by the Kilbirnie School in New Zealand where he was Governor General. We got a half day to mark the occasion and a full size flagpole was erected in front of the school. Guess what? There was never a flag on it! Eventually the pole was removed. At 5 we were dragged into Bridgend School and at 14 we broke all records leaving the school. School days were over and our bag was thrown under the bed!

## LADYLAND—1869

The starting roll was 170 with 2 teachers, Mr Fullerton and Mr McKelvie aided by pupil teachers.

In 1872, French, Music, Art, History, Geography and Cookery were taught as well as the 3 R's.

In 1900, 325 were on the school roll and the only building then was the grey building (or old school), which was surrounded by green fields, trees and an orchard.

In 1905, the head was John Fulton who encouraged the pupils to take a keen interest in nature study (it being on their doorstep), by offering a prize for the best collection of pressed flowers. Cookery classes were available but if "a girl" selected cookery extra fees were charged. By 1909, Ladyland were taking senior pupils from Bridgend and in September Mr Fulton died suddenly and Mr Ballantyne took over duties pro temp. In 1910, Mr Smith (Darkie Smith as he was known), was appointed head—he was a strict disciplinarian having trained in the army. There was a lack of accommodation and the higher classes were taught in the Templars' Hall with three supplementary classes being transferred to Central School in 1915.

In 1921, Ladyland and Bridgend Schools joined with Mr Smith as Head Teacher. Children were now able to sit exams for bursaries for secondary education, free meals were available for some of them and school desks and seats were improved—seats had backs! Central heating was installed in 1933.

The building started on the "White School" which came into use in 1937, by which time Mr Smith had retired after 43 years service to teaching, 25 years as Head at Ladyland, and Mr George Bridges took over.

***Ladyland Public School, Kilbirnie***

*Back row: J. Shaw, V. Bernardo, D. Howie, D. McLeod, D. Asbury, R. Hobbs, S. Faulds, C. Train.*
*2nd row: J. Thomson, J. Hall, W. Irvine, J. McIvor, H. Walker, J. Beigley, W. Fyfe, J. Kerr.*
*3rd row: E. Baker, F. McLean, K. Dewar, J. Dick, M. McIntyre, M. McMillan, A. Walker.*
*4th row: M. McCallum, E. Lindsay, N. Gilmour, A. Towsley, E. Reid, D. King, A. McMillan, J. Miller.*
***Ladyland 1966***

In 1948, Mr Joseph Wylie became Head and conducted many projects to swell school funds, enabling the school to buy a projector and duplicator and finance school trips. He also conducted choral singing and discovered that Kilbirnie children could sing like linnets, reinforced by many choral successes at the Ayrshire Festival.

Mrs Lang became the first woman Head at Ladyland in 1975 and transferred to Moorpark when it opened in 1978.

## MOORPARK

Moorpark was opened in 1978. This was the first of a new type of school—semi-open plan on three levels.

To begin with it was such an innovation that staff were rather apprehensive as to how teaching in this atmosphere would work. Children too found it different.

The grounds too were different, so much grass, a red blaes football pitch, in addition to the usual tarmacadam play area.

It took some time to acclimatise to this new school but everyone finally settled in well.

***Moorpark Primary***

At present, the Head Teacher is Mrs J. Gavin with a roll of 381 pupils. There are 17 teachers which includes two assistant head teachers. A visiting specialist for P.E. works with pupils in P5 and P6. A team approach chaplaincy is in operation with weekly visits to the school by the parish minister and the Salvation Army.

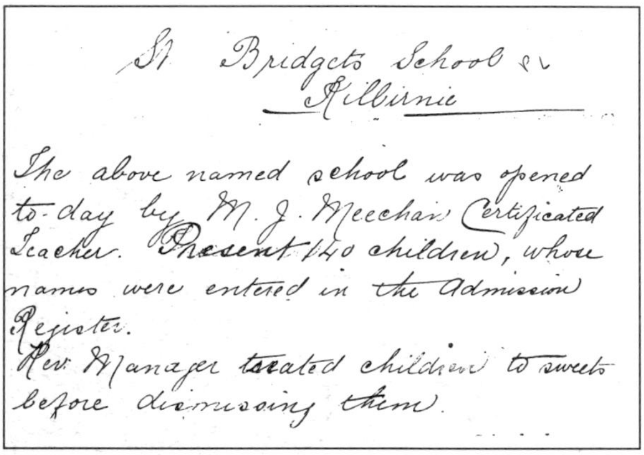
St Bridgets School &c
Kilbirnie

The above named school was opened to-day by M. J. Meechan Certificated Teacher. Present 140 children, whose names were entered in the Admission Register.
Rev. Manager treated children to sweets before dismissing them.

## ST. BRIDGET'S SCHOOL—1894

Until St. Bridget's opened, there was no Roman Catholic School. The pupils came from other schools in the district making a roll of 140.

The "Rev. Manager" mentioned in the first entry in the school log book was Rev Thomas Hopwell, Parish Priest of St. Bridget's Church which had been opened on 1st May 1862. The school was built 32 years later by the parish and at first consisted of only two classrooms erected at the top of Avil's Hill where Garnock Court Houses now stand. As the number of pupils increased, the building was added to and gradually extended down the hill to the main road—an "L" shaped building of sturdy red sandstone with four playgrounds. The lowest playground, reserved for boys football, can still be seen today with the original sandstone boundary wall at the foot of Avil's Hill about 100 yards from the Church. Catholic children travelled to school from a wide area including Lochwinnoch, Hagthorne, Glengarnock and Beith. Some walked from Beith

***Clearing the ground before building St. Bridget's school***

*St Bridget's*

*1946. St Bridget's Womens Guild Trip. Hut in the background.*

*Ist Communion 1950*

*Head Mr McIntyre with 1955 school class St Bridget's*

and Lochwinnoch—a round trip of about 6 miles a day.

In 1895, staff shortages were acute—one teacher and one monitor/senior pupil for the 150 infants! In 1897, the "New Wing" was built giving two new classrooms. In 1898, Mr James Sutherland took charge of the school and a most successful Christmas Concert was held that year. In 1899, Mr J. Fallon took over followed by Mr McGrath in 1902.

In 1915, the school received its first supply of free stationery from Kilbirnie School Board—things were tight in the school, there were only 3 teachers for 203 pupils. In 1920, senior boys were sent to Central School for woodwork and science and pupils would sit exams for bursaries to St. Michael's College (Irvine). Milk costing ½d (half penny) a bottle was issued starting in 1934, and the start of the Second World War in 1939 meant an increase in the roll due to the arrival of evacuees from Glasgow. Hot meals, cooked at Central School, were provided for 140 pupils.

In 1920, a new infants' classroom was provided in one half of an army hut which had been erected as a parish hall by the young men of the parish. This was affectionately known as "The Hut". It stood exactly where the present Library is—at the foot of the "Hut Brae"—and was the first introduction to school for hundreds of primary one children, who were lucky enough to have their play-time breaks in the public park—their unofficial playground.

A hundred years ago life in Kilbirnie was hard with much real poverty. The entry in the Log Book written by the Head Teacher on 5th August 1898 reads—

> This morning on account of weather being extremely wet and children's clothes being saturated they were sent home and there was no school.

October 30th 1899 says

> School is to be closed for three weeks on account of the Epidemic of Infectious Diseases—Measles, Typhoid Fever and Scarlet Fever.

It was closed again for 5 weeks in October 1917 for a Diptheria Epidemic during which time the school was cleaned and disinfected. These epidemics took a toll of children's lives in those days.

31st January 1908 shows the following entry:

> Free dinners, provided by St. Vincent de Paul Society, have been given daily to over 100 children whose parents have been thrown idle through the general depression of trade and scarcity of employment in Glengarnock Steel Works.

Some older parishioners still remember the General Strike of 1926 when "porridge and a scone" were given out to children before school in the morning. The porridge was made in The Walker Hall and carried in milk churns by the older boys who then competed fiercely for the job of carrying back the empty churns and bread boards as sometimes there might be a few scones left over for the "workers".

On a lighter note of excitement for the children we find:

> Wednesday 3rd June 1910—Kilbirnie Horse Fair—no holiday given out but owing to the number of horses on the road no dinner hour was given! Of course there was also the rare delight of being able to patronise the ha'penny, or even rarer, the "penny tray" in Isa McNeill's or Willie Wallace's sweetie shop on your way home from school. If you were penniless—you might know someone who had a penny and who might give you a bite of their "lucky potato" or half of their cinnamon stick!

In spite of the hard times there were two high points of great joy in the school and parish every year—First Communion Day and the St. Patrick's Day Concert.

As early as 14th November 1898 we read in the Log Book

> On Saturday evening a "Sangspeil" entitled *Round the Clock* was given by the children of the school in the hall before a crowded audience with intense success. This is the first Children's Entertainment which has been given in St. Bridget's.

An entry for March 20th 1908 reads

> A production of an Operetta entitled *Aladdin* was given by the senior children in St. Bridget's Hall. The piece was remarkably successful not only in its performance but in the crowded audience which attended to witness its performance.

These were the forerunners of the famous St. Patrick's Concerts produced by Mr Frank McIntyre, A.L.C.M., and his staff during his time at St. Bridget's. Frank had a real genius for developing dramatic and musical talent among his pupils. These concerts ran for 3 nights in March every year in the Walker Hall and involved every child and class in the school. Mr McIntyre accompanied the concert items on the piano sometimes assisted by parishioner—Mr John Girvan—on the violin. From old Concert Programmes around 1923 we find such items as *The Maypole* and the *Dainty Dancing Maidens*. An older lady in the parish still remembers singing this song in the choir about 1921:—

> The children in St. Bridget's School
> Have gathered in this hall
> To hold an entertainment
> Which we hope will please you all
> The hall is packed with people
> From ceiling to the floor
> Although they're here from far and near
> There's always room for more.

A 1937 programme shows the "Advanced Division" starring in *The Pirates of Paduff* introduced in the programme as thus:—

> Not once in our rough island story
> has toughness been the pass to glory
> See the epic struggle between Tiger McTough and
> Two-GunTeetle

This surpasses all previous spectacles . . . !

The programme for 1939 includes a musical comedy—*Redskins and Cowboys* music by Rimsky Korsakov, lyrics by Tschaikovsky! By this time the *Dainty Dancing Maidens* had progressed to the girls

***1950/51 St Patrick's Concert***

in the top classes appearing in the chorus line with two or three changes of costume in song and dance routines which would have done justice to Metro Goldwyn Mayer.

Frank used to visit the Glasgow Variety Concert Halls to get ideas for these acts and he taught all the dance steps himself!

Mr McIntyre had taken up Headship in January 1917 and was called up in August for Military Service during which he suffered a shrapnel wound which gave him his characteristic permanent, stiff legged limp—making it so easy and tempting for his more irreverent pupils to imitate—so long as he did not catch them! There have been many well loved and feared teachers in St. Bridget's. We can't list all of them so have focused on Frank McIntyre as embodying the valiant service and high educational standards which over the years they have given to the school community and which continues today in the "New" St Bridget's opened in 1963. What a character Frank was! He presided over the school for 40 years with firm discipline and authority—spice with his distinctive "dour" humour. The final Musical Production connected with him was his retiral concert in 1957—the end of an era!

It was during Mr McIntyre's Headship that St.Bridget's and all other Catholic schools in Scotland were given over to state ownership in the 1918 Education Act. St. Bridget's came under the direct management of Kilbirnie School Board thus freeing parents, for the first time, from the expense of providing for their children's books and slates.

## THE SCHOOL CONCERT

Grace Fitzsimmons recollects:—

> Many years ago, St. Bridget's School pupils held annual concerts. The children were the stars of the shows.
>
> Mr McIntyre, who was the Headmaster, played the piano and my father John Girvan played the fiddle.
>
> About 1925, Frank Rooney starred in the *Pirates of Penzance* and he played the Captain of the Pinafore.
>
> Great effort was expended on the props etc. One year, a merry-go-round featured on stage, constructed it is believed by the parents.
>
> Around 1923, the theme of the concert was the *Four Seasons* and Bunty Carrigan played "Spring". I have forgotten who played "Summer, Autumn and Winter".
>
> My father, John Girvan, was a tailor and as well as fiddling made a lot of the costumes in conjunction with the mothers of the pupils.
>
> In 1954, or thereabouts, my son Robin Fitzsimmons sang a duet with his classmate Roberta Beattie. The song was *I'm a Little Dutch Boy* and they were dressed in Dutch National Costume. After many weeks of rehearsal and preparation when they actually appeared on stage, Robin was struck dumb and failed to respond to his cue to start singing, whereupon Roberta promptly jabbed him in the ribs with her elbow to start him off.
>
> One year a relation of Mr McIntyre's—a nephew I think, who worked on a passenger liner—was visiting his uncle and was pressed into service to play his trumpet in the concert.
>
> I remember vividly the excitement on the part of the pupils and the joy of the parents when their offspring appeared on stage, all in all the happiest of memories.

In 1962, work started on building the new school in the Fudstone area with the big change over taking place in October 1963—the school was visited by many local dignitaries and very much admired—the first modern school in Kilbirnie.

## GARNOCK ACADEMY—1971

Garnock Academy was formed by the amalgamation of Beith Academy, Dalry High School, Kilbirnie Central School and Speirs School. Initially the schools operated from the four sites with each Headmaster keeping a separate log and the rector of the formed Garnock Academy keeping his. (All male this time).

Building commenced at Moorpark for the Garnock Academy and was completed by August 1972 costing one million pounds.

Transport was provided from Beith and Dalry and most departments in the school were able to proceed with normal work, to a timetable, by the 14th September. There were still some unfinished items such as blackboards to be fitted, flooring in the Gym to be completed and the lunch service to be organised!

A high percentage of pupils turned out very neatly which was very gratifying to the Rector who had not insisted on uniform.

In 1975, school councils were set up and there was a ballot among pupils for their representative, among teachers for theirs and a meeting to elect the parents' nominee.

Garnock Academy has a fine musical reputation winning awards both individually and through the North Ayrshire Youth Band.

Dr David White took over at the school as Rector in 1974 and retired April 1993.

## NEW GLENGARNOCK PRIMARY SCHOOL—1993

The new Glengarnock Primary was officially opened on 23rd March 1993 but was actually in use from May 1992. The new school has a capacity of 330 pupil places with a current roll of 288. The school is of an open plan design.

The school is positioned on a large site with landscaped grounds and a grass sports area to the rear.

The Head Teacher of the new school is Stephen Banks.

*Glengarnock Primary School*

*Opening ceremony of Garnock Academy*

*Garnock Academy*

# Picture gallery of Kilbirnie: Past and Present

## MAIN STREET

*Main Street Showing Knox Institute*

*Main Street Walking to Cross*

## MAIN STREET

*This is another view of the Main Street, showing Dick's Bakery Shop, W. W. Miller's Printing Shop, and the Old Wheat Sheaf about to be taken down; it is now empty since January 1928. Now demolished and new Post Office etc erected.*

*Jimmie Darroch's Public Hoose.*
*John Thomson's Smiddy and Jammie Law's Fish Shop below. John Thomson was a son of "Old Banff", a shoemaker and father of Uncle Davie Thomson. "Old Darroch's" was a favourite howff for old worthies.*
*A wedding reception was held here on 30th June, 1882: on this occasion Andra Darroch, Jimmie's son, brought up the pony from the stables below and walked it round Darroch's dancing hall during the wedding festivities.*

## MAIN STREET

*Main Street Showing Millers Shop*

## THE CHANGING FACES OF KILBIRNIE CROSS

*Cross prior to Picture House*

*Cross showing Picture House*

*Kilbirnie Cross*

*Good Memories*

*Main Street at Christmas*

## BRIDGEND

*Bridgend Street, Kilbirnie*

*"Ellen Broon's" (Slated) and "Jen Broon's" (Thatched)*
*Dr Hunter's lan' or tenement adjoins. "Rosie Pearson's" is in the foreground; she was famous for her "herb-beer".*
*Bridgend trees on left formed part of the garden, now the Square, finished January 1928.*

*Bridgend, Kilbirnie*

## STONYHOLM ROAD

## COCHRANE STREET AND SCHOOL WYND

*Cochrane Street, Kilbirnie*

*School Wynd, Kilbirnie*

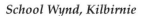

*This was the Old Parish School-Master's House, and latterly the public library was housed here. The last tenant was Mrs Hugh Davis. About one-third of the house jutted out into Schoolwynd, which it faced, and blocked the view of the North side of Cochrane Street.*
*The books in the library mentioned above were presented by the Ferguson Bequest.*

## COCHRANE STREET AND NEWTON STREET

*Peggy Livingstone's Corner to left, and Rabbie Barclay, Shoemaker's Cottage in foreground. Peggie was "Tobacco John Law's" grandmother. Free church roof in background.*

*This old house in the foreground is in Newton Street and has a date on it 1771. It adjoined a tenement known as the Saw-pit, where "John Houston's Daw" hid its thimbles and money. The Saw-pit was on the site of the present Masonic Hall.*

## GARDEN CITY AND HOLMHEAD

*Garden City, Kilbirnie*

*The Barony*

*Holmhead showing William Clark's garage*

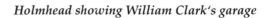

# A VIEW OF KILBIRNIE

*Bird's Eye View of Kilbirnie*

*Kilbirnie from the Bank*

## STOCKBRIDGE

*Stock Brig, River Garnock.*
*This was the old footbridge prior to the present steel one.*

*New Stockbridge, Kilbirnie*

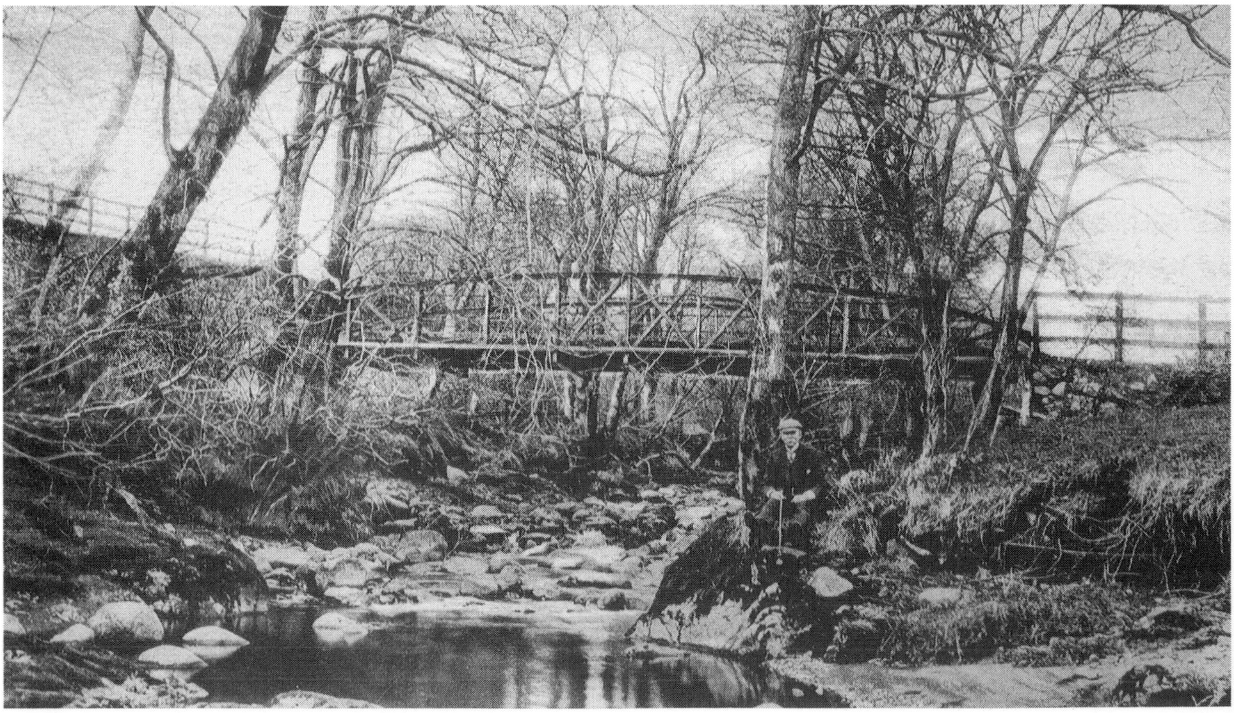

## MAICH BRIDGE AND THE BIG LINN

*Maich Bridge*

*The Big Linn on the Garnock*

## GLENGARNOCK

*Main Street, Glengarnock*

*1929*
*Butcher's Shop, Glengarnock*
*this shop is at present a cycle shop*

*Largs Road showing plots and A & D Lennox's Garage*

## KIRKLAND ROAD

*Glengarnock Station*

*"Lochview" House and Shop at Langbar about 1920. The shop has since disappeared.*

*Paraffin delivery through Dalry to Longbar*

*Newton Street Co-op*

*Craighouse Square*

*Main Street, 1953 (Coronation decorations)*

*Co-op chemist, outside and inside*

*1954 Mannequin parade, Kilbirnie Co-op Society*

*Place Pond, Garnock Castle in background*

*Watt Boys of Avinhaugh*

*Glengarnock Co-op*

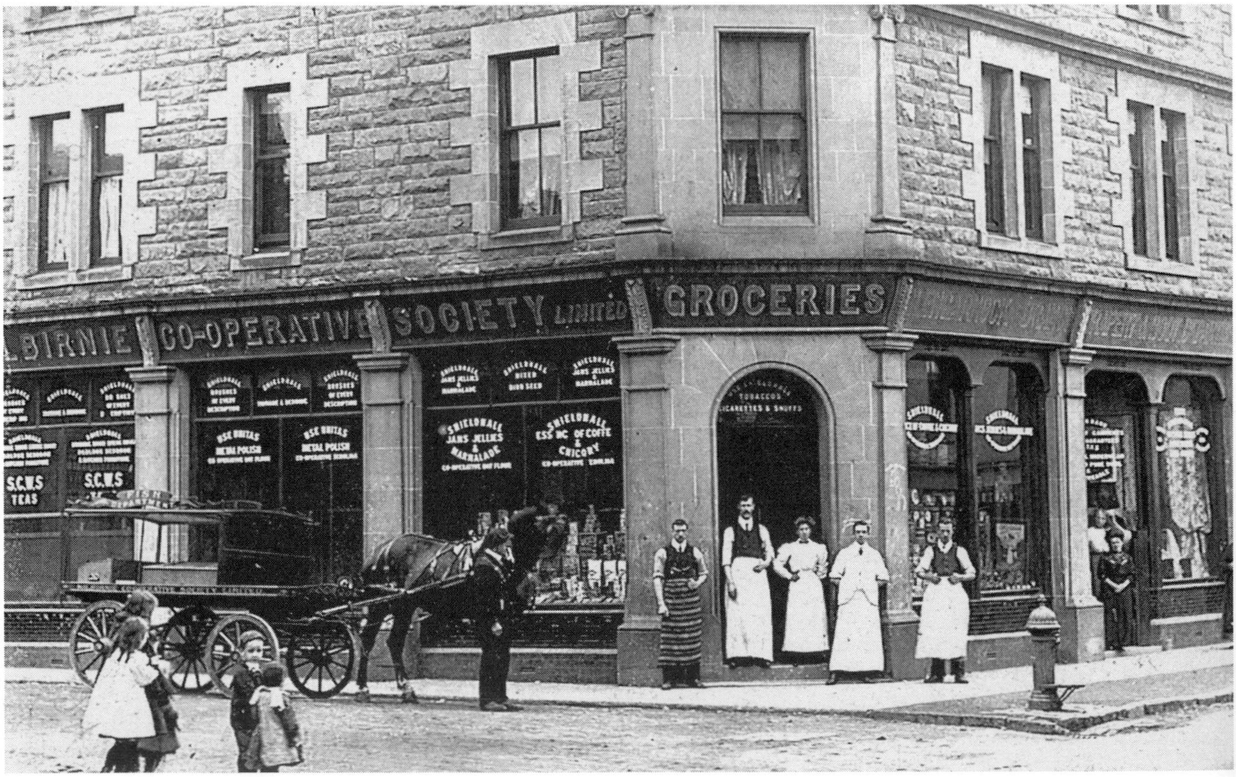

*Main Street, Kilbirnie*

*Craigend "Road". Many a child played in puddles here*

*River Garnock from Glengarnock Castle*

# Pastimes

*Local Brownie Parade at St Columbus Church*

Everyone has a hobby or interest. Bowling, football or even knitting. While trends change, the old pastimes continue on.

Kilbirnie has many clubs and organisations that flourish from year to year although this may not always be apparent to all the residents of the area!

## THE BEGINNING

For some of the children in Kilbirnie the first taste of group fellowship came with the decision at the age of 6 or 7 to join either:

**For the Boys**
Cub Scouts transferring into the Scouts *or* Anchor Boys transferring into the Boys Brigade
**For the Girls**
Rainbows transferring to Brownies then into Girl Guides *or* Ranger Guides

Anchor Boys and Rainbows have become an addition to the original groups over the last few years and they are aimed at younger children awaiting to go into the main groups.

All these organisations were well supported with various activities taking place within each different group, such as parades.

And on a less serious note everyone enjoyed outings and parties.

In 1940 1st Glengarnock Girl Guides walked to Brackenhills and collected sphagnum moss which was dried and cleaned at the lace works and then sent to the Red Cross Centre in Kilmarnock who distributed it to the war zones where it was used as cotton wool.

Sports were encouraged within the groups and teams were entered for various events with a wide range of results!

*Scout Parade at Glengarnock Church with the Rev J Houston*

*Glengarnock Girl Guides (left to right)*
***Back Row:*** *Mary Thorburn, Jean Munro, Nancy Thorburn, Grace Dailley, Jenny Struthers, Agnes Wylie*
***Middle:*** *Betty Balmer, Lizzie Martin*
***Front:*** *Alice Barrow and two evacuee's.*

## WATER WINGS

On 29th March 1969, Kilbirnie welcomed the opening of Garnock Pool by Samuel McCormack Esq. JP. The Manager, Mr Iain Blythe, was the ex Olympic Butterfly Swimmer.

Local residents flocked to use this new facility and this is reflected in the first week's attendance figures:

Adult: 2,800
Juvenile: 4,000
Spectators: 3,000

The original staff are pictured on page 58.

As well as being used by local residents, the pool was regularly used by schools in the Garnock Valley, Kilwinning, Irvine and occasionally by schools in Ardrossan, Saltcoats and Stevenston.

The building itself was designed by local architects James Houston & Son and was commissioned by Kilbirnie District Council.

The extension was added by Cunninghame District Council and was officially opened on 3rd

## Basket tea Frolics

When the Kilbirnie Boys Brigade held their recent basket tea at the Walker Memorial Halls, there was plenty of entertainment for those who attended.

Our Picture shows some of the company who provided a bit of fun at the event.

## Kilbirnie B.B. Stalwarts

Pictured below are the two Kilbirnie B.B. teams who play in the Paisley and District Battalion Leagues.

Judging by their performances, it won't be long before some of the boys are catching the eye of some juvenile club.

*Some of the original staff: George Mille, Gordon McIntosh, Jimmy McLaughlin, Agnes Lynn, David Clegg, Helen Walker, John Walker Jnr, Mary Ross and Winifred Martin.*

GLENGARNOCK
Y. M. C. A.

VAGRANTS'
DANCE . .
CLUB . . .

Membership Ticket

SESSION 1952-53

*Membership Fee 2/-*
*Charge per night 1/6*

March 1990 by David Dickie, Chairman of the Leisure Committee. This addition consisted of a leisure pool, sauna suite, two sunbed rooms and a multi-purpose room.

The final addition was in January 1992 when the multi-purpose room was converted into a fitness suite with a multi-gym and exercise bicycle.

*Right, 1st Beauty Queen (from Dalry) at Y.M.C.A*

*Fitness Room*

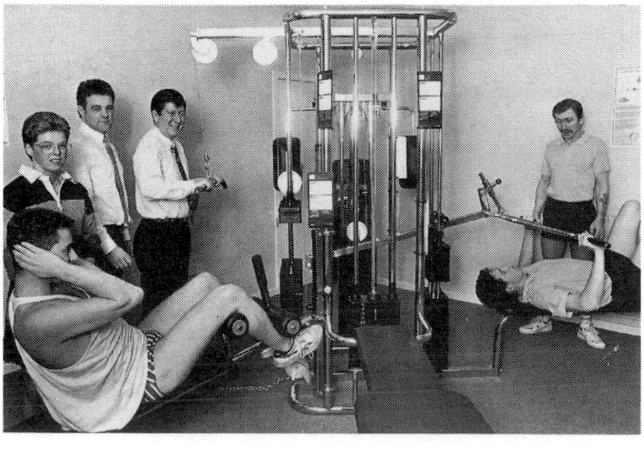

## FIT-US-IN

There were various other ways of passing the time, such as the Walker Hall Dancing on a Saturday night, or the Y.M.C.A. Vagrant's dance club where everyone enjoyed "Jigging" the night away. Many local couples will admit to having met at the local dance halls!

Monday & Tuesday, 22nd & 23rd January—
TOM NEAL, MARGO, J. CARROL NAISH in
**Behind the Rising Sun** Ⓐ
Sensational drama that rips veil from Jap terror secrets.

Wednesday & Thursday, 24th & 25th January—
GAIL PATRICK, NANCY KELLY, BILL HENRY in
**Women in Bondage** Ⓐ
It's true—it actually happened. The facts about State "control" of love. "Deputy" husbands, and the torture chamber for girls who dared to rebel.
The RADIO ROGUES with HARRY LANGDON in
**SPOTLIGHT SCANDALS** Ⓤ
Splashed with Songs and Stars.

Friday & Saturday, 26th & 27th January—
VIVIEN LEIGH, LAURENCE OLIVIER in
**Lady Hamilton** Ⓐ
Two great stars together in a grand screen feature.

Monday & Tuesday, 29th & 30th January—
KAY KYSER, ELLEN DREW, JANE WYMAN in
**My Favourite Spy** Ⓤ
The eye-dazzling music-filled comedy-romance.
TOM CONWAY, ISABEL JEWELL in
**THE 7th VICTIM** Ⓐ

Wednesday & Thursday, 31st Jan. & 1st Feb.—
To enable the many disappointed patrons who failed to gain admission on its previous visit, and to allow all who wish to see it again, we gladly bring back
**The Sullivans** Ⓤ
With ANN BAXTER and THOMAS MITCHELL.

THE
**PICTURE HOUSE**
'Phone: Beith 69—KILBIRNIE—'Phone: Beith 69

CONTINUOUS from 6.30—10.30.
SATURDAY from 6.0—10.30.
MATINEE—SATURDAY at 2.0.

ADMISSION PRICES:—
Balcony, 1/9
Back Stalls, 1/-
Front Stalls, 9d
Juveniles: 1/-, 9d & 6d

JAN., 1945

Resident Manager—J. McL. DICKIE.

**NOTE.—Entire Proceeds for Sale of Programmes go to Charity.**

Monday & Tuesday, 1st & 2nd January—
DICK POWELL, LUCILLE BALL in
**Meet the People** Ⓤ
The bright musical comedy in a brand new setting.

Wednesday & Thursday, 3rd & 4th January—
JUDY GARLAND, FREDDIE BARTHOLOMEW, with WALTER PIDGEON, MARY ASTOR in
**Listen, Darling** Ⓤ
Judy and Freddie go on a man hunt—with laughter, romance and song.

Friday & Saturday, 5th & 6th January—
IDA LUPINO, PAUL HENREID in
**In Our Time** Ⓤ
Daring, defiant, a story that could be lived only to-day, stirs the screen's deepest emotion since "Now Voyager."

Monday & Tuesday, 8th & 9th January—
LEO GORCEY and EAST SIDE KIDS in
**Mr Muggs Steps Out** Ⓐ
The screens' riotous rascals run wild in high society.
ROSEMARY LANE, JOHNNY DOWNS in
**HARVEST MELODY** Ⓤ
Lively Musical.

Wednesday & Thursday, 10th & 11th January—
ANN SHERIDAN, ROBERT CUMMINGS, RONALD REAGAN, BETTY FIELD in
**King's Row** Ⓐ
By popular demand, the return visit of an outstanding attraction.

Friday & Saturday, 12th & 13th January—
OLIVIA DE HAVILLAND, ROBERT CUMMINGS in
**Princess O'Rourke** Ⓤ
Laughter unlimited. The year's gayest comedy that won the Academy Award.

Monday & Tuesday, 15th & 16th January—
TOM NEAL, EVELYN KEYES, BRUCE BENNETT in
**There's Something About a Soldier** Ⓤ
Hearty romantic comedy drama.
PENNY SINGLETON, ARTHUR LAKE, LARRY SIMMS in **FOOTLIGHT GLAMOUR** Ⓤ

Wednesday & Thursday, 17th & 18th January—
JOSEPH COTTEN, DOLORES DEL RIO in
**Journey Into Fear** Ⓐ
It's one of the year's greatest screen thrillers
LUPE VELEZ, EDDIE ALBERT, PATSY KELLY in **LADIES' DAY** Ⓤ

Friday & Saturday, 19th & 20th January—
UNA MERKEL, DONALD NOVIS, LILLIAN CORNELL in
**Sweethearts on Parade** Ⓤ
The tuneful musical with comedy, songs, girls.
BUSTER CRABBE with FIFI D'ORSAY in
**THE JUNGLE WOMAN** Ⓐ

## FLICKS

With two well frequented picture houses in Kilbirnie, it was with great excitement that residents waited to see what would "Top the Bill" this week.

Dickie's picture house was situated where Paterson's garage now stands in Holmhead and had a wide range of pictures showing.

The Radio picture house was situated on the Cross and is now the George Bingo Hall.

The Radio Cinema was also the home to many concerts like the all star variety concert held by the Kilbirnie Auxiliary Police for the Red Cross and war work party. Special guest on 16 May 1943 was the comedian, Sir Harry Lauder.

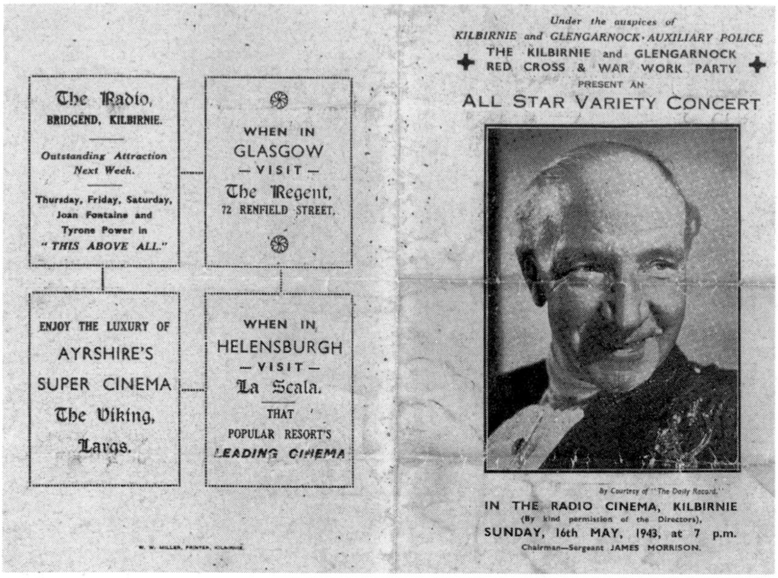

The Radio,
BRIDGEND, KILBIRNIE.

Outstanding Attraction
Next Week.

Thursday, Friday, Saturday,
Joan Fontaine and
Tyrone Power in
"THIS ABOVE ALL."

WHEN IN
GLASGOW
— VISIT —
The Regent,
72 RENFIELD STREET.

ENJOY THE LUXURY OF
AYRSHIRE'S
SUPER CINEMA
The Viking,
Largs.

WHEN IN
HELENSBURGH
— VISIT —
La Scala.
THAT
POPULAR RESORT'S
LEADING CINEMA

Under the auspices of
KILBIRNIE and GLENGARNOCK AUXILIARY POLICE
THE KILBIRNIE and GLENGARNOCK
RED CROSS & WAR WORK PARTY
PRESENT AN
ALL STAR VARIETY CONCERT

By Courtesy of "The Daily Record."

IN THE RADIO CINEMA, KILBIRNIE
(By kind permission of the Directors),
SUNDAY, 16th MAY, 1943, at 7 p.m.
Chairman—Sergeant JAMES MORRISON.

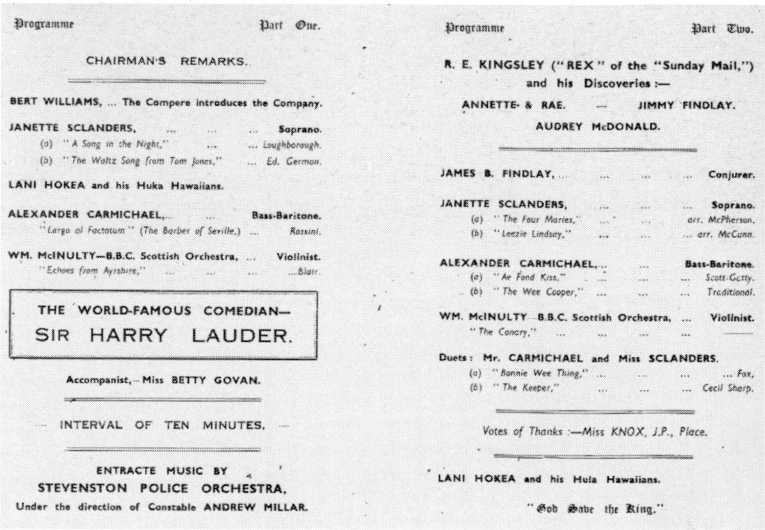

Programme — Part One.

CHAIRMAN'S REMARKS.

BERT WILLIAMS, ... The Compere introduces the Company.

JANETTE SCLANDERS, ... ... ... Soprano.
(a) "A Song in the Night," ... ... Loughborough.
(b) "The Waltz Song from Tom Jones," ... Ed. German.

LANI HOKEA and his Huka Hawaiians.

ALEXANDER CARMICHAEL, ... ... Bass-Baritone.
"Largo al Factotum" (The Barber of Seville.) ... Rossini.

WM. McINULTY—B.B.C. Scottish Orchestra, ... Violinist.
"Echoes from Ayrshire," ... ... ... ...Blair.

THE WORLD-FAMOUS COMEDIAN—
SIR HARRY LAUDER.

Accompanist,—Miss BETTY GOVAN.

INTERVAL OF TEN MINUTES.

ENTRACTE MUSIC BY
STEVENSTON POLICE ORCHESTRA,
Under the direction of Constable ANDREW MILLAR.

Programme — Part Two.

R. E. KINGSLEY ("REX" of the "Sunday Mail,")
and his Discoveries :—
ANNETTE & RAE. — JIMMY FINDLAY.
AUDREY McDONALD.

JAMES B. FINDLAY, ... ... ... ... Conjurer.

JANETTE SCLANDERS, ... ... ... Soprano.
(a) "The Four Maries," ... ... arr. McPherson.
(b) "Leezie Lindsay," ... ... ... arr. McCunn.

ALEXANDER CARMICHAEL, ... ... Bass-Baritone.
(a) "Ae Fond Kiss," ... ... ... Scott-Getty.
(b) "The Wee Cooper," ... ... ... Traditional.

WM. McINULTY B.B.C. Scottish Orchestra, ... Violinist.
"The Canary," ... ... ... ...

Duets: Mr. CARMICHAEL and Miss SCLANDERS.
(a) "Bonnie Wee Thing," ... ... ... Fox.
(b) "The Keeper," ... ... ... Cecil Sharp.

Votes of Thanks :—Miss KNOX, J.P., Place.

LANI HOKEA and his Hula Hawaiians.

"God Save the King."

This was certainly an evening worth remembering! The Radio Cinema continues to provide entertainment under its new form of the "George Bingo Hall" where the element of chance draws many to try to win their fortune!

Date of Admission — Duplicate
14/7/69 — 1628

The GEORGE
Affiliated to Telstar Link Bingo Club
Bingo & Social Club

Member's Signature.......................................
Membership Card
Strictly Not Transferable

## BANG

The local rifle club made use of the Territorial Army Hall, which is now DH Morris in Glengarnock, for their target practice and members were able to honour their club with winning the trophy.

The club was formed in 1934 and is ongoing to this day with its President being Mr McDowall. When free premises were offered by the Steelworks, the Rifle Club moved from its original location to the new meeting range in the grounds of the Steelworks and the President was the Steelworks' Manager, an Honorary position.

*Back L-R. D. McIlroy, T. Graham, A. Dick, A Lawrie.*
*Front L-R. T. Dillon, J. Gibson, A. McDonald, Robert Irvine, A. Frew.*

*The Rifle Club.*

## FORE !

Kilbirnie Place Golf Club now stands on the road leaving Kilbirnie heading to Largs.

Prior to its present position, it has had several locations and according to earliest records, the original golf course was sited on land adjoining the main road to Dalry, known to the locals as "The Briery Sink". Some years later it was moved to Brockley Hill for a short period, which was north of the present Milton Housing Estate. Its next home was land known as "The Croft" situated west of the public park now occupied by Bathville Road and part of the Fudstone Housing Scheme.

It was at "The Croft" that the first Clubhouse was built at a cost of £250. This timber building was dismantled and re-erected on the present site adjoining the first tee of the now "old" Clubhouse in 1925. This move was to 35 acres of unkept land leased at a nominal annual rent from Sir George Mathew and on his death from Miss Martha Knox. The nine holes laid out here still form part of the enlarged course.

The Club existed on limited resources from 1925 until the Second World War broke out in 1939, although many improvements and additions were made in this time.

During the war years, the club was kept alive by a small group of enthusiasts and unlike many similar sporting associations, was in a happy position to resume playing activities as and when former members and new ones returned to normal civilian occupations.

Due to strained finances, the course was maintained by the members themselves, and later a part-time greenkeeper was employed. As the

**THE NEW CLUBHOUSE**

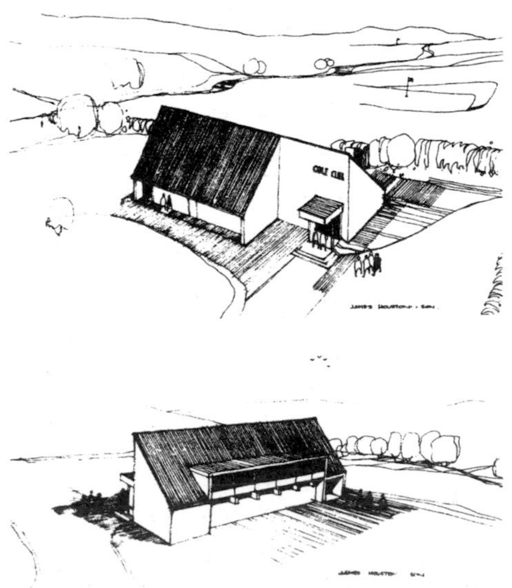

membership grew, many ground improvements took place and in August 1968 a new cedar wood Clubhouse opened to satisfy the needs of additional members. For the first time the club was able to provide a "19th Hole" service as well as other facilities which later proved inadequate for a variety of social activities.

As the waiting list for membership grew, the next step was more playing facilities. An additional 9 holes were opened in June 1977 allowing for an additional 150 members, and already plans were afoot for a new larger Clubhouse. The new Clubhouse was designed by James Houston and Son and built by James McLellan Builders Ltd.

On 10th June 1978, the new Clubhouse was officially opened with guests from various organisations including Strathclyde Regional Council, British Steel, W & J Knox Ltd, Beith Golf Club and many others.

## FLIGHT OF FANCY

The local Pigeon Club was formed in 1880 and is still going strong with members being encouraged to breed, race and train their pigeons.

The Club is affiliated to the Ayrshire Federation, the Scottish Homing Union and the National Flying Club which allows members to fly their pigeons in various competitions as well as many races and competitions being run by the club itself.

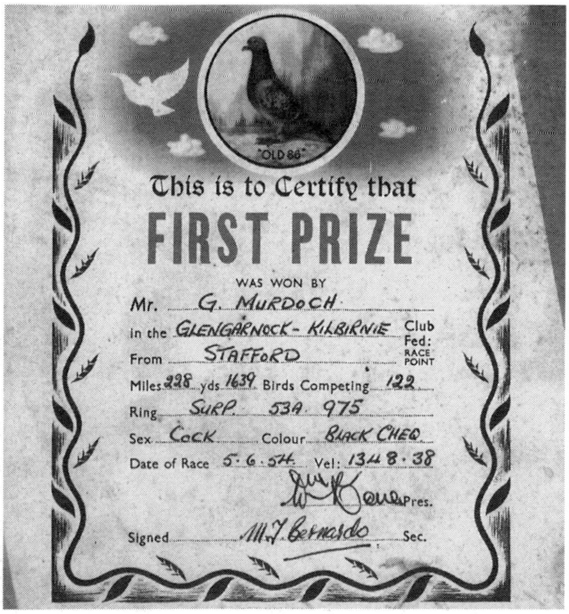
"OLD 86"
This is to Certify that
FIRST PRIZE
WAS WON BY
Mr. G. MURDOCH
in the GLENGARNOCK - KILBIRNIE Club Fed:
From STAFFORD RACE POINT
Miles 228 yds 1639 Birds Competing 122
Ring SURP. 53A 975
Sex COCK Colour BLACK CHEQ
Date of Race 5.6.54. Vel: 1348.38
Pres.
Signed M. J. Bernardo Sec.

## DOING OUR BIT!

Residents in the area have also found time to think of others in their leisure hours, organising social events for the Senior Citizens and children of the area.

The Kilbirnie and Glengarnock Common Good Committee was formed in May 1946 by six local councillors with the Dance Committee of the Forces Welcome Home Fund. The object was to provide social activities in the Kilbirnie Parish and Longbar area. By December of the year enough funds had been raised by Dance Promotions to hold the first "Old Folks Treat".

In 1947, a Children's Gala, and in 1952 the "Old Folks Summer Outing" were added to the activities and were held annually until 1959 when a court decision was announced making charities such as the Common Good liable for tax on profits.

Under these new laws, the fund was wound up and at a public meeting the same year, a new organisation, The Kilbirnie and Glengarnock Recreational and Charities Trust was formed.

Kilbirnie and Glengarnock Old People's Welfare Committee was formed from voluntary help from other organisations. It has served the Senior Citizens in the area in numerous forms from chiropody visits and clinics to grass cutting services.

This Committee was the first in Scotland to form a meals-on-wheels service and is also highly regarded for visits to the aged and infirm.

*Glengarnock Golf Club*

# Industry and Shops

Today, in 1994, we see a dramatic change in the amount and type of shops in Kilbirnie's Main Street since 1930. Gone are shops such as "The Hat Shop" and "Martin's Furniture Shop" or the Shoemaker's to be replaced by more "supermarket" type shops. One of the survivors from the 1930s is "Duncan's" whose first shop was established in 1933 and at present still have 3 shops in the town.

Industry is not quite the same as it was either with the closure of the Steelworks in 1978 and indeed the picture has changed considerably since the details below from 1837.

In 1843, Merry & Cunninghame erected 8 Blast Furnaces for the production of pig iron. The laying of the Glasgow-Ayr railway in 1840 meant that if supplies of the local black band coal, ironstone and limestone used in its production ran out, materials could be easily imported. More importantly, the pig iron could be quickly dispatched and a large trade was established with America and Europe. But as these markets began to make their own iron, and supplies of local iron became exhausted, the company decided to introduce steel making.

By 1851, the population had doubled with the influx of people to 5,494 and by 1901 it was 7,207. Glengarnock grew, families settled in the Main Street and also within the Steelworks site in rows of single storey houses. These were serviced by the company store and its liquor establishment the "Billy Ruffin"—a local pronunciation of Bellerophone—the warship that took Napoleon to exile in St Helena.

Four 8 ton Bessemer converters were installed in 1885-1920, followed in 1892 by the first open hearth furnaces, a rolling mill and a structural department.

The industry attracted families from far—Ireland, Spain, England, Italy, Poland and Lithuania—and near for the chance of

***POST***, Letters arrive from BEITH every morning at ten, and are despatched every afternoon at half-past five.

**CLERGY.**
Ferguson Rev. James (reformed presbytery), Hill cottage
Urquhart Rev. Robert (established church), Manse

**ACADEMIES AND SCHOOLS.**
Millar James, Bank [master
PAROCHIAL SCHOOL, James Muir,
Stewart James, Dennyholm

**BLACKSMITHS.**
Garven John, Newtown
Jameson John, Bridge st
Kerr John, Bridge st
Scroggie Peter, Bridge st

**BLEACHERS AND THREAD MANUFACTURERS.**
Knox William & James, Water side

**BOOT AND SHOE MAKERS.**
Allan George, Bridge st
Allan James, Newtown
Allan John, Cochran st
Anderson William, Cochran st
Irvine David, Mill st
Sinclair John, Bridge st
Steel John, Bridge st

**CARTWRIGHTS.**
Barclay James, Cochran st
Crawford Archibald, Cochran st
Dickie William, Newtown

**COTTON MANUFACTURER—BY POWER.**
Watson David, Kilbirnie mill—Matthew Shanks, manager

**FLAX SPINNERS.**
Wilson & Jamesons, Garnock mill

**FLESHERS.**
Orr Robert, Bridge st
Patton Robert, Bridge st
Shedden William, Bridge st

**GROCERS & SPIRIT DEALRS.**
Allan John, Bridge st
Brodie James, Mill st
Fife Robert (& agent), Bridge st
Fife William (tea dealer), Main st
Law John, Bridge st
Mackie James, Bridge st
Patton Robert, Bridge st
Shedden William, Bridge st
Walker James, Bridge st

**STONE MASONS.**
Knox Robert, Bridge st
Russell Allan, Bridge st

**TAILORS.**
Bryan Hugh, Main st
Clark Robert, Bridge st

**VINTNERS.**
Archibald Elizabeth, Bridge st
Crawford Robert, Bridge st
Durroch Alexander, Bridge st
Love William, Bridge st
M'Cormick Janet, Main st
Orr Robert, Bridge st
Walker John, Mill st

**Miscellaneous.**
Barclay Peter, joiner, Cochran st
Baxter Daniel, sexton
Beech Allan, tinsmith, Hamilton st
Crawford Rachael, draper, Bridge st
Dickie George, miller, Nether mill
Graham James, cabinet maker, Main st
Howie Andrew, lime burner, Auchenleck
Jameson James, coal merchant, Lade side
M'Cosh John, baker, Main st [holm
Montgomerie Skeoh, rope maker, Denny-
Orr Robt. earthenware dealer, Bridge st
Pebles James, wheel maker, Bridge st
Walker William, surgeon, Main st

***CARRIERS.***
To GLASGOW, James Allan, and James Allan, jun. every Thursday.

***Steel Workers 1930s***

employment; the men in the Steelwork and the women folk in the nearby thread and net works or the woollen mill in Dalry.

In 1890, Merry and Cunninghame's interests in the Glengarnock plant were dissolved and the Glengarnock Iron & Steel Co was formed.

From 1900-1914 there were periods of trade depression and when the war broke out in 1914 the plant was standing idle. Mr JC Cunninghame of the Glengarnock Iron & Steel Co did not feel able to restart the plant so the then Ministry of

***View of Melting Shop, Glengarnock.***

Munitions arranged that Colville & Sons would operate the plant and produce munitions of war. David Colville & Sons purchased the plant in 1916 and the plant worked at full capacity tunill the miners strike and economic collapse in 1921. In 1930, Colville & Sons amalgamated with James Dunlop & Co and became Colvilles Ltd. The works produced main girders. Locally the term Girder Shop is still used but the blast iron works had been closed in 1930 and families began to move away.

The 1930s Depression and the introduction of the Means Test meant families moving elsewhere in vain hope of work and some families lived on the "Broo money" for nigh on 5 years. Harsh conditions of the Means Test caused many people to prepare themselves in order to get a reasonable income, but the ramifications of this Means Test had violent repercussions in Kilbirnie. In February 1931, the Riot Act was read—Communist leaders, Glasgow members of the National Unemployed Workers Movement and supporters from Beith and Dalry marched to the Walker Hall where local councillors were holding a meeting. However, councillors asked the police to be there and there was a huge force of them outside the building.

The Deputation were satisfied with the answer they got but before further measures were taken, the police had drawn their batons and broke up the crowd. It is a well remembered event by older members of the Community.

The Steelworks continued to be a major employer in the Community, but by 1978 a reduced rolling mill operation employed just 200 people due to changing demands and foreign competition and the works finally closed in 1985—a major disaster for the area.

## GREEN FIELDS AND EMPTY SPACES—HUGH LAW

The death throes of the Garnock Valley's Steel Industry began in December 1978 and finally ended in the Spring of 1985. This happened despite the efforts of dedication and resolution by its workforce over many years.

Nationally and internationally this was a time of change relative to industry and its people. Locally, it was a time of trauma, as they faced unemployment on a grand scale.

For many of them, they realised that they would never work again, for many others, they'd have to move away to find work, others would have to retrain to be suitable for other industries, while many others again may return to full time education to gain new qualifications. Another option for some was to be redeployed elsewhere in the steel industry.

A nucleus of the workforce was retained at Glengarnock in 1978, and for some of them that meant working day and night to prepare the way for the mass redundancies and their subsequent effects on us all. A damning indictment perhaps; that some should profit from the misfortune of others.

The day of the redundancies dawned, and with it came a unique and unreal atmosphere. So much money, values unknown to so many, yet for all the uncertainty of the future, there was a real desire to make that Christmas special. The other restraint was to "ca' canny" and save a little for the unknown aspects of the future months. Whatever the individual viewpoint, the Co-op and other local businesses had a bumper Festive Season.

Since then, for many people, new employment has been sought and found, be it either close to home or further afield. Others have enjoyed or accepted retirement, according to age and temperament. A pension and benefit related society has emerged from one formerly wage-earning. Sadly however, unemployment continues to haunt our neighbourhood as job security has gone forever. No longer can we rely on local industry for sufficient jobs for our future generations. Such industry, as there is, cannot supply the demand as it did in years gone by. Lives have been changed drastically these last few years and our offspring in future will continually have to re-assess job prospects. The bitter taste of how Scotland's steel industry has been annihilated will linger on. People involved in steel closures like "Black Bob" Scholey and Ian McGregor will never be forgotten locally.

The former employees of Glengarnock will long remember the special friendships and relationships which were fostered within the Works. Families involved for generations as well as new-comers to the area were integrated into the Steelworks lifestyle. Beith, Dalry, Kilbirnie and beyond were all represented in Glengarnock Steelworks. Countless stories remain of many "character" employees and their exploits. At the same time, sadness too often comes to mind.

For nigh on one hundred and fifty years, that iron and steelworks was the main industry in the area.

## MRS PIPER'S RECOLLECTIONS

When I was a wee lassie there was W & J Knox, a network, in Kilbirnie. When they got very busy they would send their finished nets out to their old workers who couldn't make it into work, so my mother was one of them.

I was about 10 or 11 and I used to go to the network and get a net, put it on my back with a big reel of thread and take it home to my mother and my mother ossiled them.

The ossils were the long bits of material that the floats were put on and she cabled and run them and I'd take them back when they were finished and get another, sometimes you would get 2 to put on your back, they were big fisher nets.

My father, sister and I would fill needles for my mother to use. Then when I was 14 years old, which was a Thursday, I left the school on the

Friday and started work on the Monday in W & J Knox Linen Thread Factory.

My father spoke for me and I got a job in the finishing department where I had to lick each label and stick it on a bobbin of thread. My first wage was sixpence, then I got older and got put in the polishing department.

At that time in W & J Knox some of the girls had to stand in tubs and wash the hanks of thread in the burn. So you've got an idea what it was like in the cold days, having to break ice to wash these.

There were different departments such as the dye works, twisting and spinning and it was good material. The nets were sent abroad. Then we started making nylon nets, therefore the fishermen could cast them more than once and that's why there is only one network now where there used to be 7. There used to be a lot of work in this area. There was Dennyholm Mill, the Big Mill, the Flax Mill and the Network, now they are all flattened.

When you were a child you used to play at games such as peever, then a game we called beds, and ropes and we played with the ball—hitting it off the wall—and we gathered chestnuts. We used to follow the lamp lighter. Come night a man would come round with his pole over his shoulder, it was all gas light, and put up the light, we used to pretend that was you getting your picture taken. At Easter, we used to roll our eggs down Auchenhave, which is the big hill just outside Kilbirnie. We used to go picnics to Jacob's Well, the finest water you ever drunk.

My Dad taught us plenty of wee songs and riddles which I now teach my grandchildren, they love it.

On a Saturday night we went to the wee meeting in the Mission Hall. You got a penny to spend, half of that was on sweets before you got there. Then you got your Saturday penny which had to do a lot in those days.

In those days it was your father who cut your hair, we even made a poem about that.

When it was voting time Hunter Weston stood for this constituency. When he won the election he came through the town in a car with the hood down, we even sang a wee song about that.

It has been good looking back to when we were weans, when we had no cares and no threats of war that we knew of. We're living in terrible times just now but with prayer perhaps peace will come to this unsettled world.

## KNOX'S MILL

The Mill was established in 1778 and 216 years later is still operational and the biggest employer in Kilbirnie with over 230 workers and increasing weekly.

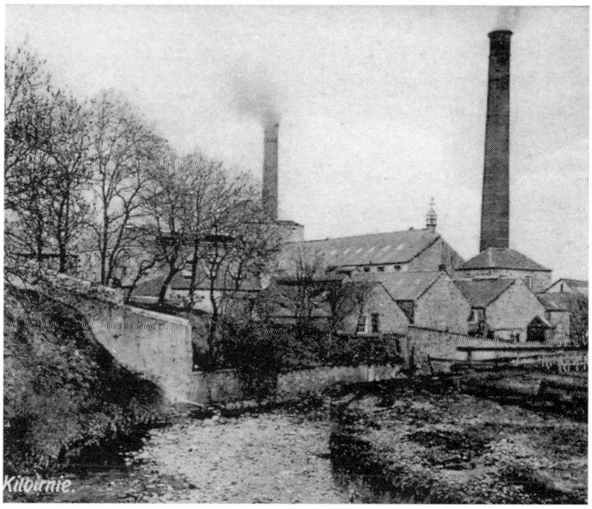


*Dennyholm Mill*

Knox's threads and nets are known all over the world and the career of the firm has been marked by continuous advancement and success. The works have been in the possession of the Knox family, their present proprietors, since their inauguration.

## EARLY HISTORY

In 1778, Robert Knox, the son of a farmer, set up a small unit for bleaching linen fabrics. At the time the main agricultural crops in the county of Ayr were oats, potatoes and flax. Robert decided to become a flax spinner, using the local crop and water power from the River Garnock. Soon he was manufacturing sewing thread for the tailoring trade and flax twine for hand-made fishing netting. His two sons, William and James, built a large five storey building to house flax machinery in 1840 and the business expanded rapidly from there on.

As specialists in hemp and flax netting twines (which increase in strength when wet) an important export business was developed in Norway (hemp twine for cod gill nets), New Zealand, where an agent was appointed ten years after Captain Cook's discovery and Canada, for flax gill nets used in Lakes Ontario and Erie. The Clyde provided regular and convenient shipping facilities.

James Knox had two sons—the elder James (later he received a Knighthood) and Bryce.

## CANADA—AN IMPORTANT MARKET FOR FLAX AND HEMP NETTING TWINES

In 1856, one of the most important customers for Knox Twines and Sewing Threads called John Leckie decided to emigrate from Glasgow to Canada. Before leaving he visited Kilbirnie where the brothers William and James Knox agreed to appoint him as agent in Upper Canada.

With his family he left the Clyde in a sailing ship, in which they arrived in Halifax, NS. Undeterred by slow travel the Leckies made their way east in a bullock cart and settled in what is now Toronto. John soon went to work among the fishing communities on the north shore of Lake Ontario—visiting his customers in a pony cart. The Knox Flax Netting Twine was already well known to the gill net fishermen and the business expanded.

Many years later in the 1920s the Knox Company acquired the Leckie family business—which had become John Leckie Limited, the leading ship chandlers with branches from St. Johns, Newfoundland, to Edmonston.

## BRITISH COLUMBIA

With the development of gill netting in B.C., the Knox Company became one of the major suppliers of flax and hemp netting twines for the hand knitting of nets. Business was conducted with the fishing companies on a direct basis and the business flourished.

In the 1880s James Knox—grandson of the founder—put into practice the family motto, "MOVEO ET PROFICIOR" when he paid his first visit to B.C.

Embarking from the Clyde in a trans-Atlantic paddle steamer (in which he was required to provide his own knife, fork and spoon) he set out on the long journey, travelling across Canada on the Canadian Pacific Railway. His luggage boasted two huge trunks, one containing his personal effects, the other boxes of Havana cigars for his customers. As he stood on the high ground, which is now Vancouver, he gazed in astonishment at the huge fleet of small gill net boats under sail, fishing offshore. He was made very welcome, not only with hospitality, but with a bulging order book—so much so that Bryce, his younger brother, sent him a telegram to stop booking further business. The factory was fully booked.

In 1898 the Knox family merged with their linen thread competitor, William Barbour and Sons, whose factory was situated in Ulster, Ireland. Trading directly with British Columbia fishing companies continued until 1934, when the Knox/ Barbour Company established the business of Western Leckie Limited in Vancouver.

## DOUBLE KNOT NETTING

Around 1900 machines became available for the manufacture of fishing nets. These were semi-automatic assisted by men or women who were required to manipulate wooded pedals with their bare feet. The machines were known as "Scotch" machines and were designed—with bobbin and shuttle—to produce herring drift nets, and only single knot netting could be made.

Bryce Knox was steeped in the manufacturing side of the business, and with foresight conceived the idea of providing double knot flax netting for Fraser River salmon. His friend, an engineer in Paris, Monsieur de Serreville, was working on the design of just such a machine, which was given the friendly name of "Bonamie". This was a fully automated machine on which the production was painfully slow—about 3 rows of netting per minute, or one and a half meshes.

The finished net was folded, wrapped in hessian and shipped to B.C. where it was mounted in the netting lofts.

The first machine-made double knot flax gill nets were supplied in the early 20s, and for years only double knot nets were acceptable in B.C.

With their Barbour partners, the Knox family became equipped with more "Bonamie" machines than all the other netting manufacturers in the world put together.

This was not their only advantage. The eldest son of Bryce Knox was called James who was an expert on the raw material i.e. flax. Before the revolution he visited Russia and set up a flax buying organisation under a Scotsman called "Jock" Houston. The flax was shipped from Riga to Dundee and thence to Kilbirnie. During both World Wars, James was responsible for the promotion of flax growing in the UK and New Zealand. The traditional flax growing countries had become battlefields.

Two major revolutions have taken place in the field of fish net manufacture:

1. The change from hand knit netting to machine knit netting in c.1900

2. The change from natural fibre to synthetic fibre in c.1952

In 1950, there was a shortage of flax double knot nets, and the Knox/Barbour companies were supplying 75% of the market.

With the application of heat, single knot gill nets could be manufactured from nylon at speed on bobbin and shuttle machines with which all net makers throughout the world were equipped. No longer was there a use for "Bonamie" and no longer was the skill of flax buying required. Competition forced the closure of Western Leckie Limited in 1960.

In spite of this, W & J Knox is still in business, enjoying an important market for nets used at fish farms, synthetic carpet yarns and work clothing.

## W & J KNOX, KILBIRNIE

### The Past 10 Years of the "Old Firm"

In 1977, 200 people in Kilbirnie were all employed in the manufacture of industrial twines and knotted fish nets for the fishing industry. Today, there are still 200 employees but only 12 people are doing a job similar to that done 10 years ago. The development of new products has been the top priority of Senior Management, a task which would have been impossible without the excellent co-operation of the workforce in Kilbirnie, who can proudly boast of being in business for over 200 years.

In 1978 Knox's main products were gill nets, both monofilament and multifilament, and trawl netting. There also was a large Twine Unit mainly used for the inhouse manufacture of twines which were later converted into nets.

The monofilament gill net was the most efficient and famous gill net ever produced. It was actually developed in Knox some 10 years before, but its success attracted the attention of the Japanese and Far Eastern countries who very quickly caught on to making this product and selling it at about half the price of the Knox UK made product. Knox's troubles were not helped at the time by the Icelandic Cod War, which put further pressure on the trawl netting section. As over 70% of production from the Knox's factory at that time was exported, and the export markets were being swallowed up by low priced imports from the Far East, Knox had to make plans for diversification.

Two opportunities arose in 1978, the first the purchase of Morrison Whyte Ltd, a carpet yarn company with factories in Irvine and Maybole, producing 40 tonnes a week of carpet yarn and employing about 120 people. The second was the starting of Knox Engineering by taking on the agency of a Japanese fish net manufacturing company.

In the next 2 years, the recession in the traditional Knox's knotted netting continued, and it was found necessary to close the Irvine and Maybole yarn factories and transfer them to Kilbirnie. Around this time, W & J Knox employed only 90 people, and the injection of the carpet yarn manufacturing company was very welcome news indeed.

Alongside this development the fish farming business of Scotland was being developed. As W & J Knox had the only knotless fish netting machines in the United Kingdom and specialised for some years in the manufacture of knotless fish nets, this product was an immediate winner when made into a fish cage for the fish farming industry.

## MR FYFFE'S RECOLLECTIONS

Mr Fyffe was born in the Coronation Building in 1902. He moved from there to a flat above the

*Wait's Network Milton Road (approx. 40-45years ago).*
*People put umbrellas up when passing here as condensation from steam came down like fine rain.*

*Lace Works—Glengarnock*

corner shop at Cochrane Street. At the age of 5 he went to Bridgend School which is now the Community Centre and he called it Ballantyne School because that was the name of the Headmaster. He then went from there to Ladyland School.

We flitted from there to Alexandra Terrace. We came home for dinner and on the way home there was often a fight with the Catholic and the Protestant. One time I lost my coat and my Mum had to go to the Catholic School to get it. We used to play Cock-a-loosy, that's where you got onto someone's back and tried to knock them down. You had to make your own entertainment. There was no Public Park, you had to play in the streets and if the police came you had to run. There wasn't as many houses then. You had to have steady work to get a house here.

In 1927, at the age of 25, I was married and had to live in a wee kitchen up by Ladyland School. It cost half a crown a week, you couldn't afford to pay 10 shillings in those days. There were about 13 of us shared the one toilet.

I left school at 14 years old to start work in the Steelworks, that was me until I stopped working. I served my time as an engineer. There were some hard times in those days. Sometimes there would be plenty of work then it wouldn't be so good. You were on a week on and a week off. I worked from 6.15am to 5.30pm. Sometimes when it was busy I would go to work on a Saturday morning at 6am and wouldn't get back home until Monday morning.

The Unemployment Agency was where the Carpet Place is now in Kilbirnie. That's what they called the Templars' Hall. There was no Walker Hall at that time and no pictures. Mr Scott, the man who had the Pictures, came once a year. It was a penny to get in. The Masonic Hall used to have dances too. The shops were open until 10pm. You would go barefoot up the roads in the summer to save your shoe leather.

I was married in the Church and afterwards we had what you used to call a bottle, a party for you and all your friends. I went to Rothesay on honeymoon. It was a lot easier to get to Rothesay then, now you have to go to Wemyss Bay to get a boat. When I went you could go from Largs. During the War we were all taken up from the Steelworks to take our particulars. The lady that took the particulars suggested the Navy for me since I was an engineer.

If the horses were in good order they were taken away for the soldiers, the others did the

*Mr Fyffe—on far right.*

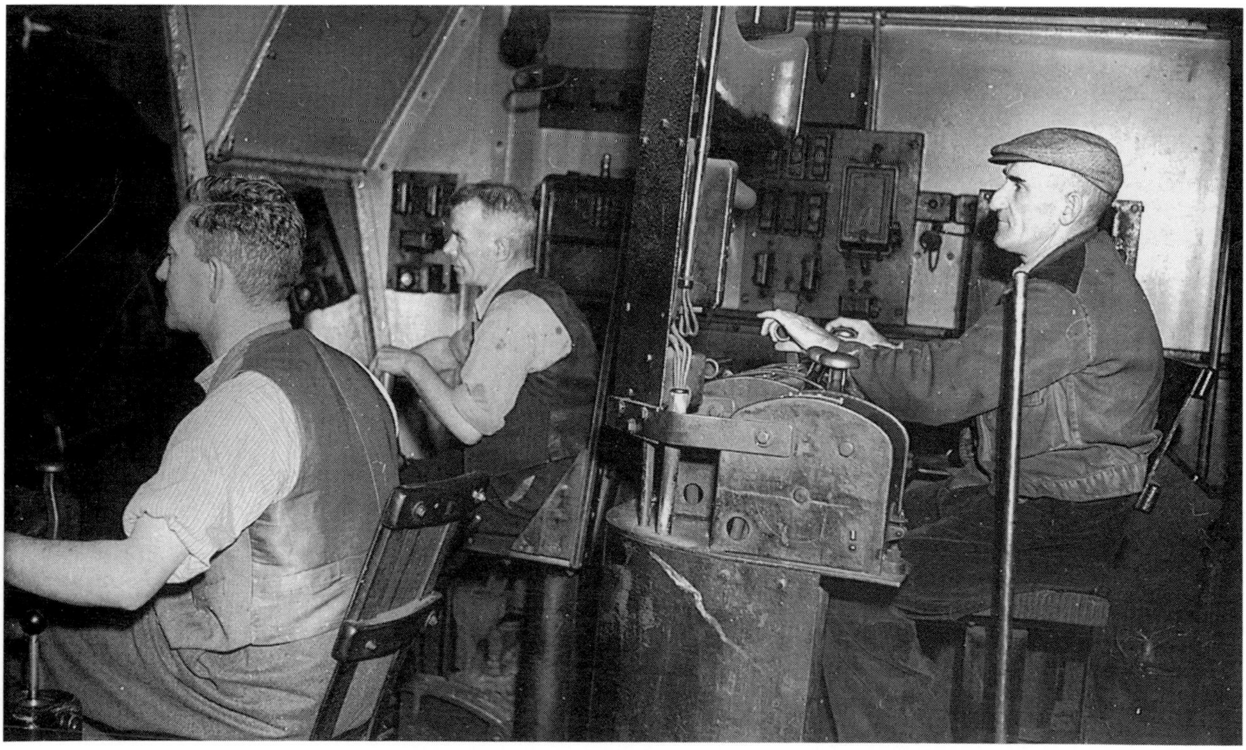

deliveries for the shops. There were wagonettes that were drawn by horses that took you to Glengarnock and Largs.

In 1927 there was an awful storm. I came home from work that night at 10pm and the storm had lifted the roof clean off the garage and knocked the wash houses down out the back door.

## MR SAUNDERSON'S RECOLLECTIONS

Mr Tom Saunderson had a grocer shop in Cochrane Street which he took over from Hugh Campbell following his return from service after World War II. Coming down Cochrane Street, Mrs Halliday had a sweet shop opposite the junction into Glasgow Street. This later was Mr Russel's hairdressers.

In Schoolwynd was the sweet shop owned by Jimmy Todd and on the other side of the road David Whiteford's butcher shop.

Turning in to Townhead we had Willy Terry the cobbler and Peggy Cook who sold a variety of goods what would commonly be known as a jenny-a-Things shop.

In Bridge Street was Jimmy Masini's ice cream parlour and chip shop, on the same side William Menzies, sweets and home baking, on the opposite side Agnes Chapman's grocers shop and Chapman butchers shop first opened in 1857, next door was Molly Boyd's sweet shop.

The first shop in Main Street was Paterson's the bakers, then Bernardo's ice cream cafe and chip shop, then the Co-operative Society, which catered for most needs:—fish shop, fruit, grocery, furnishing, bakery, butchers, drapery and shoe shop with painters, joiners, cobblers and latterly TV repairs somewhere "thro the back".

Prior to the Co-operative taking over what had been Kennedy's Hall the two front shops were the Buttercup Dairy and Polly Sloan Martin's fruit shop, them came Jossy Ireland the cobbler and Andrew Walker's licensed grocers.

Pre-war, Galbraith's store was built on the site between the two banks, then came Miss Richardson's jewellers shop next to Sally Cook's sweet shop. Her father in law was "Cook the tailor".

Then we come to our Ladies Department. The first Duncan's shop in Kilbirnie was in 1933, that was originally the Post Office. So that takes us to the cut off at Bank Street where there were houses right up there and half way up we had a sweet shop and general store.

On the opposite corner of Bank Street was

Willy Martin's furniture shop, now the TSB premises, Meikle & Co occupied what is now our gents department from 1956. Next came Singer Sewing Machine Shop run by Mrs McCarter (Lennox to her own name) and the Post Office.

The next block of shops were Miller's Bakers and Willy Taylor's chemist shop, Wilson fishmongers, Miller newagents and RS Templeton's grocer now McMaster's DIY shop. In Craighouse Square was John Barclay's joiner shop and at the corner what had been Dolly Mack's became John Miller's hairdressing salon. From there to the Masonic Hall, it was all housing other than for Robert Houston's, public house and Dougie Darroch's drapery.

Starting on the other side of Main Street we have the bingo hall, formerly the Radio Picture House opened in 1937, the architect was the present Jim Houston's father whose offices were on the original site which he sold and moved to the foot of Schoolwynd. On the east and south of the roundabout were sweet shops operated by Lizzie Crawford and Mrs Holmes, then on the corner McNeil's newagents and the Co-operative chemists, Sissie Richardson had a sweet shop and tobacconist shop before coming to William Miller's hairdressers and Tommy Jackson the jewellers.

On the other side of the Walker Hall what is now our baby shop was owned by Jessie Gemmill who retailed babywear and haberdashery, the other shop in this block was the Maybole shoe shop owned by Bob Hunter.

What is now the funeral undertakers was John Walker's bakers with the bake house under the shop, next came the Commercial Hotel owned by William Walker, now the Labour Club. The next two shops changed hands over the years, Lennox a general merchant along with Alexander's the grocers then Stevenson plumbers and Dougie Gordon solicitor and now J McCulliem's and Rock & Co solicitors.

The next block started with Archie Lennox's cycle shop, Edward McKinstry's butcher shop, Hugh Law ironmongers and John Law licensed grocer, and at the end Mancin's ice parlour and chip shop.

In Newton Street we had John Ramage publican, May Loughlin sweet shop, John Hutchinson ironmonger, Miss Mair draper with Jimmy Gallagher painter and decorator, now George Sneddon's and finally the Newton Street branch of the Co-operative Society at the end of the Jubilee Building latterly the premises of Jim Hunter, baker.

## JIM HUNTER'S RECOLLECTIONS

Shortly after the start of World War II, the firm of Craig's the joiner whose yard was at Kersland Road, Glengarnock, was taken over by a firm of boat builders by the name of A & C Head of Greenock. My father Alex Hunter, who had served his apprenticeship with Craig's and had worked with them all his days, apart from his time in the forces during World War I, was made the foreman with this new firm. Our family moved from Holmhead in Kilbirnie down to Glengarnock and lived in the house adjacent to the joinery yard.

I would guess that for the first year or so life rafts were built here. These consisted of buoyancy tanks made over with slats of wood, ropes with wooden hand grips hung all around the sides, sounds simple, but they were strongly made, they had to be to serve the purpose that they were made for! After a while, a new, long, brick built shed was added on. This was built by my father and his squad, the apprentices of course had the honour of mixing the cement by hand—no petrol mixers then—this was the place where the lifeboats would be made.

These were new skills my father and his team had to learn, and clinker built boats of a very high standard were to be produced from this yard. It was always a nice sight to see the white painted boats with their teak gunwhales being taken away on the back of a lorry. There was the odd occasion when boats would come in for repair and we would sometimes wonder what terrible times the people who had taken to them must have come through.

Tree trunks were delivered to the yard and it was our job (the apprentices) to strip the bark off them. This was done with a kind of spade (similar to the shape of a garden edging spade), a good job in the summer but a damned cold one in the winter, and the bark was harder to get off! The logs were then lifted by a crane (guess who got the job of turning the crane handle?) on to a long bogie which ran on a track, and then sawn into slabs with what was called a "German Saw", they were then cut into, I think, 4 inch by $^3/_4$ inch planks, then put through the planer. The planks were then put into a long tank of boiling water for around 2 hours, this made them pliable enough to bend into the shape of the boat. This sounds easy but it was quite a difficult job to bend the planks without breaking them. The next job was to hand rivet the planks onto ribs within the boat, this was done with copper nails and

*Shops in main Street*

***40 Main Street***

*Above: Glengarnock—Michael McGlone, J. Smith, Mrs Glen, Wullie McKelvie, Jim Pate, among others*

washers, it was a very tedious job. The tradesmen would rivet with a small hammer on the inside, while the apprentice held against the head of the nail on the outside. Surprising how many nails are in a boat! The teak gunwhales then finished off the structure, seats etc were fitted to the inside, after that came the painting and varnishing, and as said previously, on completion, the boats were taken away by lorry. Whether the boats were for the Royal or Merchant Navy I didn't know, but to my knowledge they were delivered to Greenock dockyard. That was our contribution to the war effort from the joiners in Glengarnock.

After the War, business once again changed hands, this time it was taken over oddly enough by a Mr Alex Hunter from Largs. I believe the going rumour at that time was that my father had bought it over—not so.

The work now reverted back to house joinery with the addition of furniture making. The big shed was divided into two parts for this purpose, and a partition built to separate the joinery from the furniture workshop. Another project was introduced to the yard, this was the construction of caravans for the show folk who came to Beith Fair. I remember two caravans being built, one was for Mr Johnny Swallow, I think he had roundabouts at the fair, he was an exceptionally nice person, quiet but very interesting to talk to. The other was for Billy Cullis who had a bingo stall and the patter to go with it, he was certainly a character, always ready with a joke or two. Both families were very nice.

The caravans were all hand built—no mass production here—right from the chassis, and the customers demanded and got a very high level of workmanship. The wooden framework was carefully fitted and joined together then covered with aluminium, I don't remember if they were painted at the yard or taken away to be done. The inside was then fitted out with wardrobes, dressing tables etc. These had all to be carefully measured and made in the furniture workshop, then taken to the french polishing department where the polishing was all done by hand and to a standard of the highest quality, which in my opinion would surpass anything done nowadays. The caravan was now complete.

The customer would then come with their big truck and hitch it on to the van. Once again there was a feeling of pride to see these lovely caravans, made in a small yard in Glengarnock, being towed away. To call them caravans is doing them an injustice—they were luxury homes on wheels.

It's sad when you go through Glengarnock nowadays to think at one time there was a thriving, close knit community, and a very busy Main Street. We had all the shops and services you require. Next to the railway station we had a pub (still there), Johnny Higgins, the grocer, the Co-op with all its different departments, behind the Co-op was a very industrious lacework, across the road another pub, Jessie McKelvie's sweetie shop, Jamieson the newsagent, Muir's the bakers, Daley's grocery shop and round the corner was Johnny Clark's the drapers (now the Post Office/Newsagent). Sad though it may be they tell me that's progress. I think I'll stay with my happy memories.

When my grandfather Andrew Miller came to Kilbirnie he bought Mr Dick's bakery business in 1923. There were six other bakers in Kilbirnie at that time and one in Glengarnock.

Here are some of the bakeries and their owners:

Cochrane Street Bakery: The Lightbodies, Mr Gemmell, Mr Walker and Mr Brown (after he died the bakery closed)

Mr Partridge: Mill Road

Mr Walker: Main Street

Co-operative Bakery: Muirend Street

Mr Logan who sold to Mr Paterson

Miss Faulds and Mr Menzies had a bakery in Schoolwynd only making pies and scones.

Our bakery "Miller's" was closed in 1956 and moved to an empty net-work building in Muirend Street.

At present the only bakery in Kilbirnie is within the Presto Supermarket. Two bakers have been opened, one in Main Street and the other at Bridgend, but the goods are baked outside the town.

The first Co-op bakery was behind the Co-op Central Building in the Main Street. The Co-op Muirend Street bakery was built in 1907 and employed quite a number of men and women until it closed in 1984. I think it is now a woollen store.

In my youth Kilbirnie streets were busy with delivery vans, Co-op and other bakers delivering morning rolls. At Christmas and New Year time many local women would mix and prepare their cakes and shortbread at home and then take them along to the various local bakers to have them baked in the baker's ovens as there were no electric or gas ovens in the homes then. The bakers had quite a problem getting all of the cakes baked successfully as they did not know the ingredients of each cake. Some turned out well but others failed, but of course the housewife could always blame the baker, and all for the price of 2d!

When I was young the bakers had quite a hard time, sometimes having to start as early as 2am or 3am in order to have the morning goods ready for sale. Once the process of making bread or rolls was started you had to keep at it continuously until all the goods had come out of the oven, otherwise the dough would turn sour as the yeast would continue to work in the dough. After a short break for breakfast, it was time to make pie shells, biscuits and cakes for the weekend. On Friday night we worked a nightshift starting at between 10pm and midnight in order to have a good variety of goods for sale on Saturday morning.

Modern bakers have a better life with continuous processes and up to date machinery, and I do not know if we will ever see the small baker with his bakehouse again in Kilbirnie.

In Glengarnock and Longbar there were various shops and businesses and people living there would obtain most things they wanted without having to go into Kilbirnie.

There was Higgins the Grocer on the left side looking up from the station and the Co-op with its various departments and Italian shop for ice cream and Robertson the Coal Merchant. There was a pub at the top of Burnside Street. Across the road Howieson the Draper had a shop which is now the Post Office, there was Daly the Grocer and the people enjoyed the wonderful baking smells from Jeanie Bain the baker's shop which then became Prentice the butcher shop. There was a hairdresser, tobacconist and eventually two banks opened. It's all changed now, so has the Main Street in Kilbirnie. The cinemas are away, as is Law the Ironmonger, Hutchison Ironmonger, Sally Cook's, Miss Muir the Draper amongst others to be replaced by more general stores. Presto, the Co-op and Spar Shop are supermarkets. We still have chip shops and now also Chinese takeaways and video shops and more banks and insurance brokers.

There was a library in the Longbar as well as one at Knox Institute now served by the library in Avil's Place.

Now, with regular buses, trains and more people having cars, trade is diminishing in the town as people travel further afield in search of something new or a bargain. Nothing can replace the local shop where staff know your name and always ask after you or your family.

*Glengarnock*

*Jimmie Crawford's Bake-Hoose.*
*Davie Steel was baker here before Crawford and Hughie Templeton had his Smiddy here prior to Steel: he slept in a bed in the Smiddy and was very fond of a dram.*
*This house was demolished by the Paisley Water Commissioners to make way for large water from Camphill Dam.*

*Langbar.*

Report and Balance-Sheet for Half-year ending 8th September 1954 3

# Notices to Members

## DIVIDEND ARRANGEMENTS

| | | |
|---|---|---|
| At the Regd. Office, Kilbirnie ... ... ... | TUESDAY, 26th October ... ... ... | 10 a.m. till 1 p.m., 2.30 till 5.30 p.m. |
| " " " " ... ... ... | WEDNESDAY, 27th October ... ... ... | 10 a.m. till 1 p.m., 2.30 till 5.30 p.m. |
| At Grocery Dept., Lochwinnoch ... ... ... | " " " ... ... ... | 9.30 a.m. till 12.30 p.m. |
| At the Orange Hall, Glengarnock ... ... | THURSDAY, 28th October ... ... ... | 9.30 a.m. till 12.30 p.m. |

**DIVIDENDS WILL NOT BE PAID TO CHILDREN UNDER 15 YEARS OF AGE**

**DIVIDEND WARRANT, SIGNED AND STAMPED, MUST BE PRODUCED FOR COLLECTION OF DIVIDEND**

**OFFICE HOURS:**

| | |
|---|---|
| Monday till Friday ... | 9 a.m. till 1 p.m., 2.15 till 5.30 p.m. |
| Saturday ... | 9 a.m. till 12.30 p.m. |

**SHOP HOURS: All Departments with exception of Bread and Drug Departments—**

| | |
|---|---|
| Monday, Tuesday, Thursday, Friday ... | 8 a.m. till 1 p.m., 2.15 till 6 p.m. |
| Wednesday ... | 8 a.m. till 12 noon. |
| Saturday ... | 8 a.m. till 1 p.m. |

**Drug Departments—**

| | |
|---|---|
| Monday, Tuesday, Thursday, Friday ... | 9 a.m. till 1 p.m., 2.15 till 6 p.m. |
| Wednesday ... | 9 a.m. till 12 noon. |
| Saturday ... | 9 a.m. till 1 p.m., 2.15 till 5 p.m. |
| Sunday—Central Department ... | 4.30 till 6 p.m. |
| Glengarnock Department ... | 1.45 till 2.45 p.m. |

**Bread Department—**

| | |
|---|---|
| Monday, Tuesday, Thursday, Friday ... | 6 a.m. till 1 p.m., 2.15 till 6 p.m. |
| Wednesday ... | 6 a.m. till 1 p.m., 2.15 till 5 p.m. |
| Sunday ... | 8 a.m. till 12 noon. |

**MONTHLY HOLIDAYS.**—The General Office and Shops of the Society will be closed all day on the first Wednesday in February, March, May, June, July, August, October, and November. Exception—Bread Department, open from 6 till 9.30 a.m.

**SAVINGS BANK** business is conducted at the General Office each Monday evening from 6 till 7.

**MANAGER** may be consulted at his Office on Thursday evenings between the hours of 6 and 7, or by appointment at any other time.

**BOARD OF MANAGEMENT** meet every Thursday evening at 7 o'clock.

**VAN TRADING.**—All Van accounts must be paid weekly. Members would greatly facilitate the work of vanmen by making payment in tokens on every possible occasion.

**COMPLAINTS.**—All Complaints or Suggestions should, in the first place, be referred to the charge hand of the department concerned for attention, and failing satisfaction at that point to the Managing-Secretary.

**CHANGE OF ADDRESS.**—Any Member changing address is requested to notify the Cashier immediately of the new address.

**HALF-YEAR ENDS ON 9th MARCH 1955, AT WHICH DATE ALL ACCOUNTS MUST BE CLEAR**

**SHOP AT THE CO-OP AND SAVE WHILE YOU SPEND**

Kilbirnie—2

*Report and Balance-Sheet for Half-year ending 8th September 1954*

*Glengarnock Co-op*

22nd April, 1948.

Miss Davidson,
Registrar's Department.

Longbar Library Cehtre - Glengarnock.

A Library Centre has been opened at Longbar Community Centre, Glengarnock, and the local Librarian is to be paid £10 per annum for her work as Librarian.

Will you please add her name to your list for payment and make the first payment on 15th May, 1948, for the 2 months from 16th March, 1948, and further payments thereafter as you consider suitable.

Local Librarian.
Mrs J. Cowan, (Jane Cowan)
Cochrane Lodge,
Longbar,
GLENGARNOCK.

---

10th June 55

The County Treasurer,

(Salaries and Wages)

Longbar Library Centre - Glengarnock.

Mrs J. Cowan, Cochrane Lodge, Glengarnock, has resigned her post as part-time librarian as at 15th June, 1955. Will you therefore make a payment of £5/16/8 to her now and this will settle all claims due.

Mr Neil McMillan, 20 Smith Avenue, Glengarnock, will now act as Librarian, and you might arrange to pay him in November and May each year as was the case with Mrs Cowan. The payment is at the rate of £10 per annum - £5 at each half-yearly term.

AYR COUNTY COUNCIL.

TELEGRAMS: "COUNTY, AYR."
TELEPHONE No. 2201.

ALL COMMUNICATIONS TO LIBRARIAN

County Buildings
Ayr, 22nd March, 1948.

COUNTY LIBRARY.

LONGBAR COMMUNITY CENTRE.

Instructions for the local librarian.

1. An initial supply of 350 books is sent in the following proportions:-

| | |
|---|---|
| Fiction | 300 |
| Non-Fiction | 50 |

2. A reader's card is sent for each book. This card gives the name of the Author and Title of each book. These cards should be kept in alphabetic order according to name of author.

---

Rules for issuing books.

1. Enter the name of the borrower on the card for the book which is being borrowed together with the date on which it is borrowed. When the book is returned, the date of return should be entered in the appropriate column and the book can then be issued to another borrower. Care should be taken to ensure that the books are not returned to the book shelves, or given to another intending borrower, before being marked off as returned.

2. A typed list of the books is sent with this first lot of books. Thereafter, this list will be revised and sent after the books have been exchanged.

Exchange of a portion of the book stock.

1. In order not to breal the continuity of the service, a proportion only of the books will be exchanged at specified intervals. Due notice of this exchange will be given and an indication of the number of books to be withdrawn and packed up for collection will be given. For each book being returned, the relative reader' card must be returned. These cards are required for purpose of recording issue and MUST always be used when thebooks are issued.

It shall be closed on Sundays, Christmas Day, New Year's Day, Local Holidays, and any other time the Committee may from time to time determine. Should any alteration to the above be necessary, notices intimating such changes will be displayed in the Library.

2. Books may be borrowed by any person 12 years of age and over and application forms may be had from the Librarian. Electors whose names appear on the current Register of Electors may borrow books on their own responsibility. Non-Electors must have their form signed by an elector.

3. Readers shall be held responsible for any damage done to books while in their possession, and are requested to report any defect or damage in any book.

4. Readers should report any case of infectious disease occurring in the house while a library book is in their possession, and they may not use the Library until the house has been declared free from infection.

5. Fourteen days are allowed for reading a book but it may be renewed for another period if no demand has been made for it by any other reader. If not returned within the time a fine of one penny per week or portion of a week shall be charged for each volume.

6. Any particular book may be reserved on application to the Librarian by payment of one penny for postal charges. A post card will be sent when the book is available.

7. Readers are requested to intimate any change of address, and on ceasing to use the Library to hand over tickets to be cancelled.

# Churches of Kilbirnie

## THE AULD KIRK

There has been a church in Kilbirnie since about 500 AD when it is reputed that St Brendan or St Birnius set up his cell to convert the pagan natives, who were possibly those who were living on the Crannog on the loch. Since then, the Auld Kirk in Kilbirnie has grown piecemeal, much of it under the auspices of Sir John Crawfurd of Place who had a burial vault built for the "Crawfurd Gallery" which is possibly unique in Scotland. The Laird's Loft is highly carved and embellished along the front with armorial bearings of John Crawfurd, the first Viscount Garnock. The Laird and his family sat at the front and behind the screen were seats for his servants with a shut off pen at the side of the gallery for the cook, who could easily slip out during the sermon to prepare a meal in the kitchen, which now serves as the vestry.

This beautifully carved gallery is recalled in this account by Captain Arthur C Crawfurd:

> My mother having died when I was a child, I was brought up under the ennobling influence of my aunt, Mrs Hunter of Hunterston, my mother's eldest sister, nee Crawfurd of Cartsburn. Her sister lived in the neighbourhood of Ardrossan, and it was the delight of the two families to meet as often as possible for divine service at the old Kilbirnie Kirk.
>
> There we sat in the beautiful carved Crawfurd Gallery, and often after a very long service and a longer sermon, we used to adjourn to the chamber behind the gallery (now the vestry), where the lunch was served and where we sat 'till the afternoon service commenced, equally long and very trying for a boy with a restless disposition.Often I have been carried out

*Parish Church, From the South*

of that gallery and well thrashed by my uncle in the churchyard, and then returned for a continuation of the service. My aunts did their best to keep me quiet with repeated doses of sweets, but it always ended in my being forcibly removed and chastised.

*Crauford Gallery, Parish Church, Kilbirnie*

The pulpit is one of the oldest wood carvings in the church, dating to about 1620, and is carved with many symbolic representations. Over it is the canopy, decorated also with many symbols including the "Angel of the Annunciation" holding an olive wand and standing on coiled serpents.

When the new gallery was built in 1903, it too was embellished with panels of the Heritors, indicating their professions. Rev Lachlan Watt describes the church as "The most beautiful church ever seen".

There are many other carvings and memorials throughout the church including the lovely stained glass windows. Sanctus Birnius is portrayed in the one inserted in the north wall of the church. In 1990 a new memorial stained glass window was installed to commemorate the church's 500th Anniversary.

In the churchyard are some very early graves reputed to be of crusaders because of particular features carved on them. Also, among the graves of past ministers and past members of the church is the Crawfurd Mausoleum, erected in 1594 by Captain Thomas Crawfurd of Jordanhill. He and his wife are not buried within, but are buried to the north side of it. Through the small window can be seen the effigies of the Captain and his wife.

The Auld Kirk has had many other names such as The Barony Church, and has seen many changes in its life. Other churches sprang up around the town accommodating other Christian denominations.

The present minister of the Auld Kirk is the Rev Douglas Irving.

## GLENGARNOCK CHURCH

The congregation comprising of Kilbirnie, Beith, Longbar and Glengarnock "folks" was formed in 1870, and together they raised the funds to build the church a few years later. It was originally United Presbyterian, becoming United Free Church and after the union of the churches in 1929 became Glengarnock Parish Church. It has had 5 ministers before the union with the Barony Church, namely Mr Gray, Mr Andrew, Mr Mackie, Mr Dempster and Rev Mr J Houston. The close liaison with Glengarnock Steelworks can be seen with the appointment of Rev J Houston as their Chaplain. With the retiral of the Rev Houston in 1978, the church joined with the Barony to form the Auld Kirk of Kilbirnie. When the church was demolished in the winter of 1989 a lead time capsule was dug up with coins, newspapers and other items of the time. This is now in safe keeping in the Auld Kirk.

On the demolition of the church, the bell tower was donated to the village via Jackie Clark by Mr Lygate who had purchased the land for the erection of two houses. Mr Clark raised the funds to lay the bell tower in the centre of Glengarnock, which was completed in 1992, in memory of the church. The church bell itself was donated to a mission in Zambia.

The church hall, built in 1931, has been converted and is now used as a centre for arts, crafts and education. Now it is called the Valley ARC.

**KILBIRNIE WEST CHURCH**

Before 1825, the people of the Reformed Presbyterian congregation met in houses, fields and barns, or walked to Kilmacolm to worship. William Orr of Kilbirnie Place has been named as the driving force behind the proposal for a congregation led from Kilbirnie with their own minister, and the original building was opened on 20th April 1825. The first minister to be appointed was Rev James Ferguson. In the statistical account of 1841, the West Church had the only Sunday School in the area and had a library for the use of the congregation. In 1876, the reformed Presbyterian Church united with the Free Church and the church was now called the West Free Church. (It faced the East Free Church and both churches worked happily side by side until they joined.)

A new church building was opened for worship on 7th July 1889 and was called locally The Red Kirk because of the red sandstone with which it was built. Shortly after, three stained glass windows were installed to the memory of William Knox of Moorpark, George Knox of Redheugh and James Knox of Riverside, representatives of the family which had been associated with the congregation from the start. The congregation was eventually absorbed into the United Free Church around the beginning of the century and in 1929 became a congregation of the National Church.

In 1924, a small book was compiled on the history of the United Free Church to commemorate the 100th birthday celebration of the church, 1824-1924.

In 1964, the West Church joined with the East Church to become St Columba's Parish Church. The present minister is Rev David Broster.

**KILBIRNIE EAST CHURCH**

This church, the White Church, was directly opposite the West Church in Glasgow Street. It came into being in 1843 and is renowned for its evangelical endeavours in Britain and overseas. The congregation came from the "disruption" in the 1840s when half the ministers at the General Assembly formed themselves into the Free Church of Scotland. After 1964, it became the main place of worship, and the West Church became a very beautiful and useful church hall.

*Kilbirnie East Church*

## ST BRIGID'S CHAPEL

Prior to 1843, there were very few Roman Catholics in Kilbirnie, but after the construction of the blast furnaces at the ironworks, many people came into the town to work there. Many of the tenants of the rows and tenements of the ironworks were Irish immigrants and even from as far afield as Poland. At this time, Kilbirnie was a "station" of Dalry, where the resident priest lived. He came to Kilbirnie to the mass centre which was held in a local hall in Main Street, Tam Kennedy's Hall, where 34 Main Street is now. Father Sheedy from Barrhead, Father John McDermott from Campbeltown and Father John Tuohy from Glasgow were pioneers in Catholicism in Kilbirnie.

The Chapel still has the notebook kept by Father McDermott in which he kept record of his marriages and baptisms. The first marriage by Father McDermott was that of Margaret McMahon and John Quinn (both of Kilbirnie) on 1st November 1845. Baptisms in Kilbirnie start on January 25th 1846 with the baptism of John, son of John Donnelly and Mary Coleman.

*St Brigid's Chapel, Kilbirnie*

In 1859, Father Thomas P Lee became the first resident priest in Kilbirnie. His parish included Lochwinnoch and Beith. By this time Tam Kennedy's Hall was far too small for its purpose, and 11th May 1862 saw the opening service of the Chapel built on ground called Avilshill. The church was a modest Gothic structure with plain exterior. It was built as a simple rectangle and could seat 500 people. It had a gallery, a porch, a vestry and a confessional. There was no other building there until the industrial school in 1865.

Father Angelo Celetti was the second resident priest and came from Italy. His chief concern was the education of the children, and he set up Sunday Schools, Day Schools and Night Schools for their instruction. St Bridget's School was completed in May 1884 by Father Thomas Hopewell at the other end of Avilshill. Father Hopewell was a tireless worker for the community, working on the school board from its beginning. In 1920, a church hall was built where Kilbirnie Library is today. The congregation grew and by the 1950 the church was again too small. The decision was made to extend and refurbish the present church as opposed to building anew, and the restored church was opened by Father McGee on Sunday 2nd June 1957.

The main alteration in the interior was the attractively plain altar set against a most unusual background of blue. Two new confessionals, new side doors and an altar recessed into the south wall. An extension was added to the west wing of the existing church providing a new sanctuary and sacristy with accommodation for the altar boys. At the other end a spacious new baptistry and a one-door porch were grafted to the old structure. The extensions and modernisations were the work of architect Mr James Houston. The church celebrated its "Centenary" on 13 May 1962 with the production of a souvenir brochure covering the history of the church. The present priest is Father Tosh.

## HEBRON HALL—CHRISTIAN BRETHREN

Around 1900, a hall known as "Duffield's Building" stood on the Glengarnock side of Grey School. There were Gospel meetings and Sunday School worshipped here for many years.

When the Orange Hall was built the meetings and Sunday School transferred to here. During the first World War, when David Colville took over the Steelworks, a number of families came down from Motherwell and they helped with the work in the Gospel meetings and Sunday School.

There was also a Sunday School held in the Steelworks in a room known as the "Reading Room", and it was the Christians from the Gospel Hall who taught the boys and girls in attendance.

In November 1918, the Christians in Glengarnock started an assembly meeting in the Orange Hall. There were about 50 people in attendance at this time. In 1920, a plot of ground was purchased from David Colville and building commenced on the "Hebron Hall" as we know it now. The hall was built by people in the meeting and was all voluntary work. They worked five days a week and on a Saturday they walked to Largs to hold open air meetings. They had a fellowship of over 100 people and approximately 250 children attended the Sunday School when the hall opened in 1921.

In 1937, the Longbar "Housing Scheme" was completed and the Hebron Hall assembly purchased a building known as "The Stables" from Ayr County. This was renovated and Gospel meetings, Sunday School and Bible Class were carried out here until about the middle of the War until it had to stop due to the depletion of workers.

Ayr County bought the Hall back and it was now Longbar Community Centre.

Sadly we look at our depleted number of children present and think fondly back to our annual outings when the Longbar children and the children from the Hebron Hall would go on the train to the "seashore", usually being Ardrossan, Troon, Stevenston or Ayr, and of the fun and laughter enjoyed by all.

*Kilbirnie Young People's Band, 1924 (Band Leader Robert Irvine)*

## SALVATION ARMY—KILBIRNIE CORPS

The Kilbirnie Corps came into being in June 1892 and although the first meetings were held at various locations in the town, the first official hall or meeting place was a small building in Townhead commonly known by local Salvationists as the "Old Barracks".

The first Salvation Army Officer to command the Corps was Lieutenant Polly Tandrum.

In 1919, the Corps moved to larger premises in Milton Road, commonly known as the "Tim Hut" but it served a happy useful purpose. This area is now the site of the local Presto supermarket.

The present Citadel was built and an extension added to the rear to accommodate the work with the young people.

The Corps formed special links with the Redheugh Adolescent Unit which was opened by the Salvation Army in 1953.

Unfortunately, the adolescent work has now ceased, but a thriving "Day Care Centre" operates from Redheugh.

## GOSPEL HALL

In 1882, there was a visit made to Kilbirnie by the "Blue Ribbon Gospel Army", an evangelical and temperance group of women intent upon sharing the gospel with others. They held meetings in the Good Templers' Hall and despite opposition large companies gathered to hear the gospel. When the campaign ended those converted continued to meet for their gospel witness and study of the word of God in "Martin's Shed". (Opposite the car park on Townhead Street).

In 1897, the assembly was called together to discuss the feasibility of purchasing the piece of land on which the Gospel Hall now stands. It was agreed that the elders should go ahead with the project and they were successful in acquiring the site.

On 17th April 1897, the Gospel Hall was opened.

In 1912, a bible class was begun. Open air meetings were held on Sunday evenings. There was also a Tuesday evening open air meeting at Craighouse Square.

# Clubs and Societies

**TO A MOUSE**

Kilbirnie and Glengarnock residents are great admirers of the Scots bard Robert (Rabbie) Burns, and there are two main Burns Clubs in the area.

Garnock Burns Club was founded in the year 1867 with the object of the Club being "to promote social intercourse among the members and the study and improvement of the knowledge and works of the poet Robert Burns."

The membership charge was 1/- on admission in 1867 and was increased in 1909 to an annual subscription of six pence.

The club is still in being and has met for the Supper every year with the exception of the years from 1915-1920. The membership is limited to 30 members but guests can be accommodated.

The Supper was held in the Anderson's Pub in Cochrane Street, Kilbirnie from the year 1900 until 1980 continuously. The cost of the Supper originally in 1896 was 2/- (i.e. 10p).

A Special Meeting was held on the 20th January 1967 to celebrate 100 years of the Club and was held in the Milton Hotel. The President at this time was Mr William Clark and the Chairman was Mr William Johnston.

The members in the early years were all from Kilbirnie and the names are still well known.

PROGRAMME

Chairman: Mr. William Johnstone

Toast ..... ..... ..... The Royal Family
Mr. W. Clark (H), President

'GOD SAVE THE QUEEN'

| | |
|---|---|
| Welcome to New Members | Mr. W. Martin |
| Toast—'Imperial Forces' | Mr. D. Doris |
| Song—'Rule Brittania' | The Company |
| Recitation | Mr. A. MacGregor |
| Reply | Mr. D. McLelland |
| Song—'There was a lad' | Mr. F. I. Willis & Company |

**'Immortal Memory'**
Mr. W. Clark (H)

| | |
|---|---|
| Club Memoirs & Laureation | Mr. W. Baxter |
| Lass o' Ballochmyle | Mr. D. McLelland |

**'Jean Armour'**
Mr. R. Houston

| | |
|---|---|
| Recitation | Mr. J. Walker |
| Song | Mr. R. Melville |
| Departed Member | Mr. W. Johnston |
| Toast—'Town & Trade' | Mr. W. Martin |
| Cameo | Mr. W. Johnston |
| Reply | Mr. J. Irvine |
| Song—'Ye Banks and Braes' | The Company |

Maestro: Mr. John Law

**"The Haggis"**
"Fair fa' your honest sonsie face,
Great Chieftain o' the puddin' race."
Mr. R. Houston

| | |
|---|---|
| Song ..... ..... ..... | Mr. W. Law |
| " ..... ..... ..... | Mr. R. Davies |
| " ..... ..... ..... | Mr. R.S. Skillen |
| Reply—New Members ..... | Mr. J. Porter |
| Song ..... ..... ..... | Mr. W. Clark (L) |
| " ..... ..... ..... | Mr. S.J. Hamilton |
| " ..... ..... ..... | Mr. J. Clark |
| " ..... ..... ..... | Mr. R. Reekie |
| " ..... ..... ..... | Mr. I. Morrison |
| " ..... ..... ..... | Mr. H. Walker |
| " ..... ..... ..... | Mr. Wilson Anderson |
| " ..... ..... ..... | Mr. J. Downes |
| " ..... ..... ..... | Mr. S. Thomson |
| " ..... ..... ..... | Mr. J. Upton |
| " ..... ..... ..... | Mr. J. M. Henderson |
| " ..... ..... ..... | Mr. Wm. Anderson |
| " ..... ..... ..... | Mr. A.C. Stevenson |
| " ..... ..... ..... | Mr. J. Jackson |

"Votes of Thanks"
Mr. W. Jamieson

**"Auld Lang Syne"**

Chairman
President
Croupier
SBC/Treas
Guest

GARNOCK BURNS CLUB
INSTITUTED 1868

# ONE HUNDREDTH Anniversary Meeting

Held in

The Milton Hotel, Cochrane Street,
KILBIRNIE

Friday 20th. January — Nineteen Sixty-Seven

## *Programme and Toast List.*

Toast, - - "King, Queen and Royal Family."
PRESIDENT.

Song, - - - "God Save the King."
COMPANY.

Toast, - "Army, Navy and Reserve Forces."
PRESIDENT.

Song, - - - - "Rule Britannia."
COMPANY.

Reply—Mr. H. McTaggart.

Song, - - - - - "Scots wha hae."
Mr. Wm. Shaw.

**"THE IMMORTAL MEMORY,"--President.**

A last request, permit me here,
When yearly ye assemble a',
Ae roun' I ask it wi' a tear,
Tae him the Bard that's faur awa'.

Song, - - - - "There was a Lad."
Mr. R. F. McIlroy.

Recitation, - "The Ronalds of the Bennals."
Mr. J. McMurdo.

**"JEAN ARMOUR,"--Vice-President.**

Song, - - - - - "Of a' the airts."
Mr. James Barclay.

Song, - - - "The Lass o' Ballochmyle."
Mr. William Clark.

Song, - - "The Braes o' Ballochmyle."
Mr. G. Guthrie.

Song, - - - - "Mary Morrison,"
Mr. J. McGill.

Song, - - - - "Afton Water."
Mr. John Barclay.

Song, - - - - "Go, fetch to me."
Mr. John Clark.

**"ADDRESS TO A HAGGIS,"--President.**

Song, - - "When the moon is on the heather."
Mr. R. F. McIlroy.

Remarks—Mr. Jas. Gillies.

Song, - - - - "Open the door."
Mr. N. Reid.

Song, - - - - "Bonnie wee thing."
Mr. James Barclay.

Recitation, - - - Tam o' Shanter."
Mr. Jas. Clark.

Song, - - - - "The Lea Rig."
Vice-President.

Song. - - - - "Scotland Yet."
Mr. Wm. Walker.

Song, - - - - - "Senora."
Mr. John Gillies.

Recitation, - - "Man was made to mourn."
Mr. Wm. Tod.

Song, - - - - "My Nannie's awa'."
Mr. Wm. Curlett.

Song, - - - - "The Deil's awa'."
Mr. Wm. Shaw.

Trio, - - - - - - Selected.

Toast, - - - - - - "Our Host."
Mr. James Gillies.

Reply, - - - Mr. G. Grant.

"Should auld acquaintance be forgot."
Company.

The Rosebury Burns Club was formed in 1906 with the first "Anniversary Getherin" held in Bridgend Vaults, on 25th O'Jan'war, 1906 at 7 o'clock at night shairp! The Chairman being Mr Watt of the Firbank. The Annual Burn's Supper is the highlight of the year.

## MASONS

The Masonic Club was founded in 1859 as No. 399. The membership has grown steadily with Masons from all walks of life, and in as far away places as Canada and New Zealand.

The Masons used to meet in Miller's Hall, but in 1904 moved to their present site in the Masonic Hall where a social club has since been opened.

The ladies section, the Eastern Star, also meets in the hall.

## KILBIRNIE LADESIDE FOOTBALL CLUB

Kilbirnie, it is true, is "Fitba Crazy!" With a team like Ladeside, they have a right to be proud!

Kilbirnie Ladeside Football Club was founded in 1901 when their home ground was situated off Mill Road. They remained until after World War II.

The club itself was named after the stream, the Lade, which ran by the side of their home park.

During the War, the park was used as a base for the armed forces, at which time it was badly damaged leaving Kilbirnie Ladeside without a playing field. As their greatest rivals, Glengarnock Thistle, did not reform after the War, Ladeside moved to their ground at Thistle Valefield which remains their current home.

Playing in amber and black, the "bumblebees" as they have been known have achieved many successes and made the club's 50th Anniversary

*Masonic Lodge, Kilbirnie*

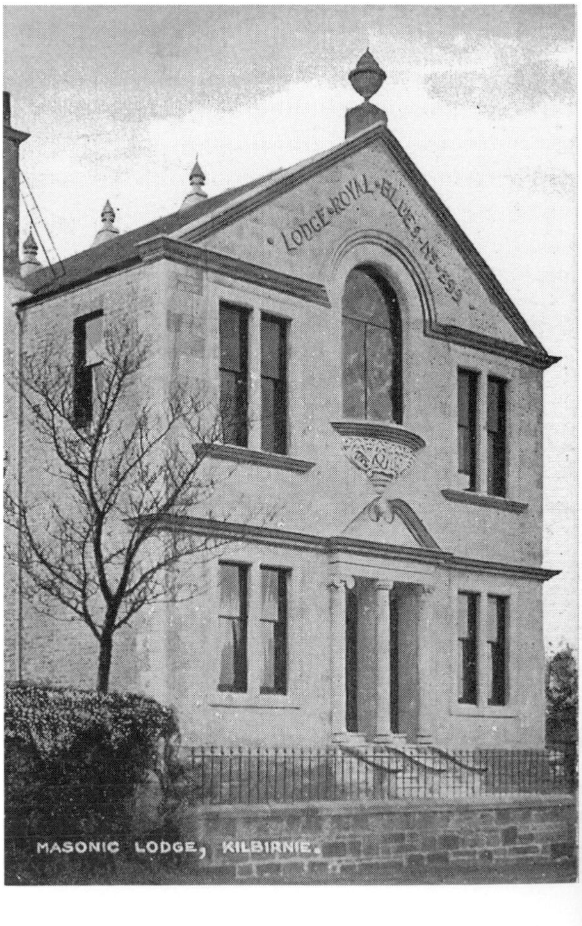

in 1951-52 a season to remember by winning the Scottish Junior Cup at Hampden Park, beating Camelon 1 goal to 0.

In 1977, they beat Kirkintilloch Rob Roy by 3 goals to 1 and won the Scottish Junior Cup once again. The greatest honour a junior club can receive.

## AMATEUR FOOTBALL

Not only does Kilbirnie have a good junior football team, but there have been several amateur teams to remember such as Kilbirnie Garnock Glenvale, Glengarnock YMCA and Colville's United.

Colville's United made it to the top of the Ayrshire Second Division League Table for the season 1959-60.

## THE JETS

In 1987, the Jets FC were founded with Archie McIntyre as President and Jim Duffield as Manager. In their four years as a Sunday team, in the Irvine and District League, the Jets lifted six trophies all under the Captaincy of John "Sconie" Davidson.

In 1991, the Jets moved to the Ayrshire Amateur Association to continue their quest for trophies as a Saturday team. Again, "Sconie" Davidson was to lift a trophy as the Jets won the Third Division.

With help from Graham and Debbie of Rascals Bar, Margaret Gunion of Jeden Carpets and the Masonic Arms, the Jets were starting to gain some security as well as a reputation for entertaining football.

Season 1993-94 saw the Jets finish as runners up in the Second Division but more importantly, they were promoted to the First Division.

Now the Jets were in with the big boys and season 1993-94, the Jets finished 5th in the League and were narrowly beaten by one goal in the Ayrshire Cup by Knockentiber.

Season 1994-95 awaits the Jets as a respected First Division team, also the beginning of the Jets Boys Club under 14s which will be joining the Central Ayrshire League.

## KILBIRNIE ANGLING CLUB

The Angling Club was founded in 1904 when it then fished Kilbirnie Loch and the Plan Dam (Pundeavon reservoir). The membership stood at 100.

Competitions were regularly held on club waters plus the Camphill Reservoir, courtesy of the Paisley Water Commission who annually gave the club 25 permits for one of the competitions—places were drawn for ballot for this—a normal prize would be half a crown!

*Colville's United season 1952-53, Lumley Cup Final*

*Colville's United, season 1952-53. Lumley Cup Final*

*First Season amateurs Jets pictured with the Kelburn Cup, which they collected for winning the North Third Division title.*

9

LEAGUE TABLES, 1959-60

North 1st Division

| | P. | W. | D. | L. | F. | A, | Pts |
|---|---|---|---|---|---|---|---|
| Girdle Toll | 22 | 17 | 0 | 5 | 71 | 40 | 34 |
| Dirrans Ath. | 22 | 15 | 3 | 4 | 70 | 33 | 33 |
| West Kilbride | 22 | 16 | 1 | 5 | 72 | 41 | 33 |
| Ramblos Ams. | 22 | 16 | 0 | 6 | 79 | 49 | 32 |
| Eglinton Ams. | 22 | 12 | 4 | 6 | 60 | 33 | 28 |
| Star of the Sea | 22 | 14 | 0 | 8 | 66 | 47 | 28 |
| Templand Rovers | 22 | 11 | 2 | 9 | 68 | 53 | 24 |
| Ard. Winton Ams. | 22 | 8 | 2 | 12 | 58 | 59 | 18 |
| Shell Ams. | 22 | 5 | 1 | 16 | 41 | 71 | 11 |
| Wilson Ath. | 22 | 5 | 1 | 16 | 45 | 84 | 11 |
| Dreghorn Ams. | 22 | 4 | 1 | 17 | 35 | 90 | 9 |
| Springside Ams. | 22 | 1 | 1 | 20 | 17 | 82 | 3 |

2nd Division

| | | | | | | | |
|---|---|---|---|---|---|---|---|
| Colville's Un. | 16 | 16 | 0 | 0 | 89 | 16 | 32 |
| Largs Ams. | 16 | 12 | 2 | 2 | 49 | 24 | 26 |
| Stevenston Un. | 16 | 9 | 2 | 5 | 39 | 28 | 20 |
| Crosshouse Wav. | 16 | 7 | 4 | 5 | 45 | 32 | 18 |
| St. Paul's Ams. | 16 | 6 | 2 | 8 | 32 | 49 | 14 |
| Auchenharvie Rvs. | 16 | 5 | 1 | 10 | 44 | 46 | 11 |
| Kelburn Rvs. | 16 | 4 | 2 | 10 | 25 | 75 | 10 |
| Kerr's Ath. | 16 | 3 | 1 | 12 | 23 | 21 | 7 |
| Corsehill Un. | 16 | 3 | 0 | 13 | 18 | 73 | 6 |

The Muirend Reservoir had a hatchery, and in May 1929, 500 yearling brown trout were purchased for the sum of £12 10/- and the club received a discount of 12/6 for prompt payment.

In 1931 the membership stood at 125 with an annual fee of 3/-. In 1932 the fee was reduced to 2/6 and at the AGM the club decided that only one rod should be in use at any one time. A law that still stands today!

In September 1933 the William Houston Cup was donated to the club and was fished for as the championship cup in 1934 and is still in use to this day for the same competition.

In 1934 Mr John Blair was approached with regard to the possibility of the club fishing the Dubbs Water. This was agreed and fishing began in the newly acquired waters.

1937 saw Mr A McDowall being presented with a silver fish for winning the championship William Houston Cup for three consecutive years.

In 1984 £525 compensation was received to restore the loch from Strathclyde following pollution of the river Garnock at Kilbirnie Cross.

*Back Row (Left to Right)—Willie Calderwood, -?, - Johnston, Sanny McDowall (treasurer), - ?, - Laughland, Willie Weir, Mungo McLelland (Co-op Cobbler).*
*Front Row (Left to Right)—Willie Martin, (at one time treasurer), - "Farmer" Hynds, John Turnbull, Willie Walker.*

## GLENGARNOCK IRONWORKS BOWLING CLUB

At the inauguration of Glengarnock Ironworks Bowling Club in 1858, the first president appointed was Mr John Jack, and as no other records are available it would appear he held office till 1900. He was succeeded by Mr EJW Richards who held office till 1911. He was in turn succeeded by Mr Lewis J Pearson from 1912 till 1914.

It would appear as if a committee was then formed and a different president appointed each year. Even during WW I this continued with Messrs Gavin Riddet, Andrew Harris, Hames Daly and Robert Cunningham holding the office annually till 1919. The following held the office until 1924 when the bowling green was resited at its present situation at Lochend Road. Messrs Daniel Logan, John Drysdale, PA Abernethy, James Vann and John McGhie.

With the bowling green now in site but still affiliated to Glengarnock Steelworks most of its members were either steel workers or resident in the vicinity of the "hill" and Glengarnock.

The president for 1950 was Andrew Johnstone. Andrew is still a playing member at Glengarnock, although his sight doesn't allow him to participate like he would wish. He will be well known to a lot of readers.

GLENGARNOCK WORKS BOWLING CLUB CENTENARY

1959 was an exceptional year in that the male and female presidents were husband and wife, James and Mary Cardwell.

The Glengarnock Bowling Club has always been a friendly family club; if you look through the names appended the same family names keep recurring. Glengarnock was the last "valley" club to incorporate a bar, as it had until the closure of the steelworks, never needed one. Glengarnock prior to 1954 had for some time a bowling touring team which used to tour in Ireland.

***Mrs J Sharp, wife of the president, throws the first jack to open Glengarnock Bowling Club in 1972.***

## LADIES SECTION

After the Second World War, women were gradually allowed to play on the Glengarnock bowling green. This did not always meet with the male members' approval, but a female section was eventually formed, which seemed to have gone defunct about 1954, and was resurrected again in 1959, with the first lady president being Mary Cardwell.

The most successful lady was Mrs Mulholland—10 times champion since 1978. She won the Ayrshire Secretary Championship in 1975, and further represented Scotland at the Commonwealth Games on several occasions. Other honours were the Ladies West Trophy in 1967 and the Ayrshire Rinks in 1966 and 1971.

## LADESIDE OF KILBIRNIE

The Bowling Club opened on 25th August 1860 and at this point you were not "a member" but a "shareholder" of the club. The number of shareholders stood at approximately 30.

The land which the green stood on belonged to Mr W. Jamieson who resided at Ladeside House, Mill Road, Kilbirnie. The fee levied by Mr Jamieson was £4.00 per year to rent the land. Shareholders paid £1.00 per share.

In 1900, W.J. Knox took over the land and over the years the membership grew. The title deeds of the club were handed over to the office bearers in 1968 and in 1976 they purchased the land.

On completion of the new club house in 1978, members transferred from the old building to the new one which had cost the club £57,000 to build.

The membership to date stands at a total of 150 male and female. Mr J Lang who was the Ayrshire Bowling Champion is still a member to this day.

The Club is a social gathering point, not only in the bowling season but during the winter months many members get together for a quiet drink, a game of pool or just a good old "blether".

## GARNOCK RUGBY FOOTBALL CLUB
### *(formerly Old Spierian Football Club)*

Colours: Green, Old Gold and Black.
Ground: Lochshore, Glengarnock, Beith.

The Club owes its existence to the late Mr R. Bruce Lockhart, the first Headmaster of Spiers School, Beith, and a former Vice President of the Scottish Rugby Union. The School opened on 22nd September, 1888. *The Scottish Referee* of 19th November, 1888 reports:

> A Rugby club has started in connection with Spiers School, Beith. The idea originated with Mr R. Bruce Lockhart, who is an old rugby player, having played for the last 18 years, stopping last winter. He played in the 1884/85/86 for Royal High School F.P., scoring the highest number of tries for season 1884/85 when J.P. Veitch was

captain. Mr Lockhart is Headmaster of this new school.

Spiers School thus became the first School in the West of Scotland outwith Glasgow and Greenock to play the game of Rugby Football. The first game between the School XV and Old Boys side took place at the School ground Marshalland on 30th October, 1890, the School winning by one try to nil. However, the Old Spierian Football Club (later Old Spierian Rugby Club) was not founded until ten years later in 1900. The first match was played against Craigielea who were defeated by one goal to nil.

For the next few years the club carried on with varying success but due to lack of support was forced to suspend activities in 1907.

The club was revived in 1911 and admitted to the Scottish Football Union on 7th March of that year as "Old Spierian Football Club".

With the closure of Spiers School in 1971 and nearby Dalry High School losing its status as a Senior Secondary School, it was decided that the club change its name to Garnock Rugby Club.

Since 1972 Garnock R.F.C. continued to play at Marshalland and at Dalry Public Park but recently were instigators in the setting up of Garnock Valley Community Sports Club where they now use high standard playing fields and clubhouse accommodation.

Garnock played in the 4th Division of the National Leagues but with no local schools continuing to play rugby, attracting players became more and more difficult as time passed and in successive seasons from 1982 to 1986 the club First XV were relegated and dropped into the 1st Division of the Glasgow District League. Garnock were top of this League in the Season 1986/87 and are currently playing in the 7th Division of the National Leagues.

Former Old Spierians who were capped for Scotland were Dr Alexander Frew in 1901, J.H. Bruce Lockhart in 1913 and 1920 and David Shedden 15 times between 1972 and 1978.

## GARNOCK CHORAL SOCIETY

Steelworkers having a break for their piece, and a choral society making music, don't seem to have much in common, but just after the first world war the Colvilles Steel men had their own festival of music, and Glengarnock workers decided to enter the competitive field. Thus at meal breaks, with a tuning fork, they formed a choir of male singers. The results created by this group were overwhelming and a pride and joy to all the locals. One of the adjudicators at the Colville's Festivals was Sir Hugh Robertson of Glasgow Phoenix fame.

By the year 1921, the decision was made to include the ladies, and so a new mixed voice choir was formed under the name of the Garnock Choral Society. Since the choir was founded it has continued in its existence with an unbroken link in making music.

Over the years, the Choral has achieved many notable successes at music festivals held in Kilmarnock, Ayr, Greenock and Glasgow. One of these occasions was when they won the Bardrochat Trophy at Ayr in the early 1930s and also brought home the festival banner for the most outstanding performance covering the whole festival.

At the Scottish Industrial Exhibition of 1964 the Choral were invited to take part in the festival of choirs at the Kelvin Hall, Glasgow and as well as taking part in the competition, they also performed for part of one of the concerts.

Another regular feature was the choir's participation in the BBC radio programme 'Scotland Sings'.

An annual concert is held in the Walker Memorial Hall, Kilbirnie, in April, at which guest artistes of note also take part. Special celebration concerts took place to mark the 50th and 70th Anniversary.

# Transport

During the 1950s, many different forms of transport were available.

## BUSES

Young Buses operated a service between Glasgow-West Kilbride-Seamill in the summer.

The SMT Buses operated several services from Glasgow to Ayr, Ardrossan and Largs.

Some of these services operated via Lochwinnoch Road which would have been useful for people who were using Kilbirnie Railway Station.

Walker's Buses operated a local service between Kilbirnie and Beith. The garage was next to the Masonic Lodge on Newton Street at the bottom of Walkers Brae.

Walker's Buses were based at Walker's Garage, Newton Street and Walker's Street.

*Young's Bus*

This route was eventually operated by Garnock Valley Buses which was eventually replaced by Paterson's buses who already operated a local route in Dalry.

*Our 1st Local "Bus"*

*Our Wee Locals!*

## RAILWAY STATIONS

There were two main railway stations in the area, Kilbirnie and Glengarnock. Kilbirnie Station was used more by people living in that part of town as Glengarnock was not really accessible. The main entrance was in Lochwinnoch Road. Some parts of the platforms are still intact.

The station was closed down during the 1960s leaving only Glengarnock Station.

This station was much busier, serving not only local people from Glengarnock but also those from Kilbirnie who lived in that end of town.

There was a separate station in Beith.

*Glengarnock Station prior to modernisation*

## TAXIS

Walker's Buses had a taxi service as well as the bus service in the area.

The Co-op also provided a taxi service for funerals.

*Kilbirnie Station (Caley) Stoneyholm Road*

## TRANSPORT TODAY

Today paints an entirely different picture of transport in the community with only one railway station at Glengarnock.

The Glasgow to Ardrossan bus service has been limited and only a few buses each day go to Paisley. However the Beith-Kilbirnie service to Kilmarnock operates regularly for people going to Crosshouse Hospital.

The deregulation of the bus service has meant more services in Ayrshire which includes a local service from Beith to Saltcoats. Also a service operates from Kilbirnie to Crosshouse Hospital starting in Milton Quadrant.

Clydeside 2000 is now an employee owned company providing a service to Largs from Glasgow as well as a local service.

Twice a day it also operates express coaches to and from Glasgow. Paterson and Brown still operate the local service, just as they have for some years now.

*Garnock Valley*

# Decades of Change

## DIVISION OF LAND

The parish was owned by three families. The three baronies were Kilbirnie, Glengarnock and Ladyland.

In 1742 the houses were lit by gas, making Kilbirnie the smallest town in Scotland to have this facility. There were farms and houses on the estates but Kilbirnie was cut off from travellers because of lack of roads.

There were roads nearby but one branched at the Kerse to Beith and the other from Largs turned at the Hourat towards Dalry. Kilbirnie's reputation as a place of "rough manners and uncouth speech" did little to enhance visits from strangers. In 1766 a new road was built from the Mill district in Johnstone through Lochwinnoch coming into Kilbirnie at Bridgend. This meant that mill owners from Glasgow and Paisley could make use of local workers and thus Kilbirnie began to grow rapidly as a small centre of mills. Mill owners housed workers in specially built houses in Dennyholm or new streets like Cochrane Street, Glasgow Street of Montgomerieston and by 1820 this end of the town was a little village of grey stone built houses with blue slate roofs.

At the other end of the town, ore had been found and Merry and Allison who had obtained mineral rights to all ironstone bands grew with the advent of the new railway. This railway ran alongside Kilbirnie Loch which meant fuel could be transported if the local coal couldn't suffice.

The erection of blast furnaces by Merry and Cunninghame caused the rise of the village now called Glengarnock then known as Kilbirnie Ironworks.

In 1845 in the new tenements and housing rows, the population was about 1,000 and the other village near Kilbirnie Station housed workers in the wool mills and chemical works.

Incomers, desperate for work, would accept any housing available. The 'Raws' were rows of one-storey single ends. They were waterless, insanitary, overcrowded with no amenities and the only lighting came from paraffin lamps. Slop water was poured into 'Sheughs' which were open channels at the front of the houses and rubbish put into "Mickeys" or ashpits nearby. There was limited room for furniture and most had set-in beds, under which people stored their coal.

There were 31 Ironstone Mines in the Garnock Valley and alongside the running of the mills and millhouses other changes were taking place. The laird of Kilbirnie was encouraging tenants on the estates to set up for themselves. By 1860 Kilbirnie had become a sort of trading burgh and people also stayed in places like the Den (Borestone). The houses at the Boston were frequently flooded by the burn and the tenants often consoled themselves at Gibby Sharp's pub.

The Mills had decided the positioning of the shops in Kilbirnie. The Steelworks brought Glengarnock and Ironstone mines brought the outlying rows. Over the years minor changes filled in blank areas and formed a line of houses from Daisybank to the Cross.

Those who became rich moved from mill houses and built rural mansions like the Place, Moorpark and Redheugh while people who had business in Glasgow built sturdy houses in Stoneyholm Road to be near the railway station (Caledonian). In 1917 Covilles built houses in Garden City for better off employees—an attempt at a suburb.

By the early 1900s, descendants of the mill workers couldn't wait to get out of the raws and since the employers were unlikely to build enough houses, the new idea of housing schemes seemed the answer. These were houses built with government money and rented out by local authorities and by the end of the first World War housing schemes were beginning to form all over the country, reaching Kilbirnie by the 1920s. Between the Wars, Glenriddet was built, then came the Milton and Prefabs in 1949 followed by the Fudstone in 1956. Kilbirnie was changing shape as all these schemes were built outwith the old boundaries.

Private housing developments began to spring up around the 1960s with individual dwellings being built in Geirston Road, then again in the 1970s with Herriot Avenue, which was started by K C Construction and finished by Wimpey and Dipple Court.

In 1977 the first sheltered housing complex, Montgomerie Court, was built on the site of the old Caley Station. This consisted of 24 individual houses and 18 residential bedrooms linked to a common support unit.

Connell Court Sheltered Housing followed on 4 March 1984.

In 1990 the old Co-op building at the Cross was knocked down and replaced with new houses including a new rent/leisure office replacing the old rent office which had been in the old Police Station. The original "Co Nock" (Clock) has been incorporated into the exterior of the building.

Recent developments are the L & C Estate on the Largs road and the Wimpey estate on the site of Dennyholm Mill behind where the "Jubilee Building", demolished in 1992, stood.

Kilbirnie will continue to develop and change but hopefully still maintain memories of old histories whilst generating new ones.

## BARONY OF KILBIRNIE

This was the most extensive of the three and occupied the south and most fertile quarter of the parish. It consisted of 5500 acres almost 3000 of which were arable, meadow and woodland. At one time this belonged to the Barclays of Ardrossan.

In 1470 the last of the Barclays married Malcolm Crawfurd of Greenock, founder of the Crawfurds of Kilbirnie. Their descendants were in the land for over two hundred years.

John Crawfurd, who had no sons, died in 1661 leaving two daughters. The younger married the second son of the fourteenth Earl of Crawfurd.

Their eldest son was made Viscount Mount Crawfurd by Queen Anne in 1703. He later changed this to Garnock in 1708 to be known as Viscount Garnock.

## BARONY OF GLENGARNOCK

This consisted of 1400 acres of which more than 1000 acres was excellent arable land.

The most ancient possessors were the Riddels, one of the oldest Scottish families. Very little is actually known about this family except that an Heiress married Harvey Cunninghame of Kilmaurs prior to 1266. He is supposed to have fought at the Battle of Largs in 1263.

The second son of this marriage was the ancestor of the Cunninghames of Glengarnock.

## BARONY OF LADYLAND

This occupied the north quarter of the Parish. There were 1800 acres, half of which was arable. The rest was pasture and moorland.

Nothing is known about the ancient owners. Prior to 1564 it had been acquired by a branch of the Barclays of Kilbirnie.

David Barclay, the successor, was arrested in 1592 for conspiracy. He was imprisoned in Glasgow but escaped and went to Spain. In 1597, he returned and went to Ailsa Craig where he drowned.

It is interesting to note that he was friendly with Montgomery the poet. David Barclay was also a poet; two of his sonnets have survived.

The Barclays sold Ladyland in 1620.

## THE DEN

Yin afternin I took a walk, frae Beith doon tae the Den,
Tw'as there I spent some happy days, but its many years since then,
The place its maist deserted noo, there's jist a hoose or twa,
The office and the store are doon, and they hinna left a raw.

I daunert up the road a wee, and stood and lucket roon,
I couldna see a soul about, nor could I hear a soon.
An o' the Den is gey sair chinged, frae the Den that I hae seen,
When the pits were gaun an' the wee Flit Baun an' a senior fitba team.

The House that Jack built's stinnin yet, but noo it is the Co.,
The wee shop that Allan kept is doon long long ago.
The big Lawn's gone an' the Cobblers Shop, and Granny Walkers work
An' the wee Schill Raw its doon an a', that stood fornent the kirk.

The Auld Hoose is stinnin yet, we kent it best by Pugs,
But there's no a buddy rinnin noo, wi bottles or wi jugs.
For noo its lost its license, an' there's no a drap ava,
Though miny a bottle has been selt, through the wee hole in the wa'.

Up on the know at last I sclimed, an' stood an' lucked roon,
On the Meidow Heid, the Maulside an' the dear auld Boolin Green.
Then I turned roon the ither way, an' see the same auld schill,
But there's no a wain gaun tae it noo, an' aw the place is still.

When we were callans at the schill, an' got our holidays,
We ran about the heather moss, or up on Rabbie's Braes.
An' in Bumbo we had a dook, or up some bing would sclim,
Then hungry we would hurry hame, an' doon the Cullhill rin.

The happy days have lang since gone, we're no sae young ye ken,
When past our sixtieth milestone we're nearing journeys end,
An' noo am feeling kinda stiff, bit a wis soople then,
When I played fitba in the BA Alley, wae the callants o' the Den.

Of the old folk I remember, like the hooses now all gone,
With thier weird and wonderous nicknames, still their memory lingers
There was Stulty Bell, an' Fish Kate, Laddelty an' Lum,
The Cobbler, The Butcher, The Sailor an' Pug Young.

There was Tam the warmer CooCoo, Pluffy Deans an' Tam the Baker,
Auld Ooorie, an' Bummer, now all gone to their Maker.
An' as I stand at the corner, as I do now an' then,
It makes me very proud to say, I was born in the DEN.

# AYR COUNTY COUNCIL

1962 - 63

## TENANT'S RENT CARD

This Card is the property of Ayr County Council

REPAIRS. All matters pertaining to repairs should be reported to the Housing Inspector on his periodical visits. Where a matter of urgency arises (e.g. burst pipe, etc.) notification should be sent to :—

*Works Manager :* COUNTY COUNCIL WORKS DEPARTMENT, 23 ST. LEONARD'S ROAD, AYR
Tel. No. AYR 66781

Tenants must not assume that every repair reported by them as necessary will, in fact, be carried out.

**IMPORTANT.—It is essential that this Card be produced when a payment is made.**

POSTAL REMITTANCES. These must be accompanied by Rent Card and return postage.

*County Treasurer* HENRY KERR, A.A.C.C.A. COUNTY BUILDINGS, AYR

All correspondence in regard to charges should be addressed to the County Treasurer. Correspondence in connection with tenancy matters should be addressed to the County Clerk.

951159 Alfred Gilbert & Sons, Ltd., London, N.W.9 •••••• D2-176-61

When making payment please see that all entries are made by Rent Collector in duplicate through the Special Collection Sheet provided. ANY OTHER KIND OF ENTRY IS NOT OFFICIAL.

The dates below show the periods of collection. During these periods the Rent Collector will call at the house. If payment is not made to the Collector on his visit the charges will be shown as in arrears.

| Fortnight Ending | Amount Paid | | | Received By | | Ref. No. Ho. | St. | Arrears Car'd Fwd | Ho. No. / St. No. / Fort. No. |
|---|---|---|---|---|---|---|---|---|---|
| 1962 B Fwd. | | | | | | | | | |
| May 28 | | | | | | | | | 1 |
| June 11 | | | | | | | | | 2 |
| ,, 25 | | | | | | | | | 3 |
| July 9 | | | | | | | | | 4 |
| ,, 23 | | | | | | | | | 5 |
| Aug. 6 | | | | | | | | | 6 |
| ,, 20 | | | | | | | | | 7 |
| Sept 3 | | | | | 2. | 12/1 | | | 8 |
| ,, 17 | 2 | 12 | 1 | | 4/9 | 2 | 633 | | 9 |
| Oct. 1 | 1 | 1 | 6 | | 26/9 | 3 | 633 | | 10 |
| ,, 15 | 2 | 2 | 11 | | 12/10 | 3 | 633 | | 11 |
| ,, 29 | 2 | 2 | 11 | | 26/10 | 3 | 633 | | 12 |
| Nov 12 | 2 | 7 | 7 | | 9/11 | 633 | 3 | | 13 |
| ,, 26 | 2 | 2 | 11 | | 23/11 | 3 | 633 | | 14 |
| Dec. 10 | 2 | 2 | 11 | | 7/12 | 3 | 633 | | 15 |
| ,, 24 | 2 | 2 | 11 | | 21/12 | 3 | 633 | | 16 |
| 1963 Jan. 7 | | | | | | | | | 17 |
| ,, 21 | 3 | 4 | 4 | | 18/1 | 3 | 633 | | 18 |
| Feb. 4 | 2 | 2 | 11 | | 1/2 | 3 | 633 | | 19 |
| ,, 18 | 2 | 2 | 11 | | 15/2 | 3 | 633 | | 20 |
| Mar. 4 | 2 | 2 | 11 | | 1/3 | 3 | 633 | | 21 |
| ,, 18 | 2 | 2 | 11 | | 15/3 | 3 | 633 | | 22 |
| Apr. 1 | 2 | 2 | 11 | | 29/3 | 3 | 633 | | 23 |
| ,, 15 | 2 | 2 | 11 | | 12/4 | 3 | 633 | | 24 |
| ,, 29 | 2 | 2 | 11 | | 26/4 | 3 | 633 | | 25 |
| May 13 | 2 | 2 | 11 | | 10/5 | 3 | 633 | | 26 |
| TOTAL | | | | | | | | | |

...ded in each collection, tenants should divide the amount shown in "rent" column by 24 (in case of four weekly collection divide by 12)

•••••• D2-177-61

ASSESSMENTS. At the commencement of each year an estimate will be made of the rates due on your house and the amount due at each collection will be fixed as a provisional figure. During the year the rent card will be recalled and the actual amount of rates for the year inserted and the amount per collection adjusted. This will be done as required by the County Treasurer.

Any appeal against rates, whether on the grounds of poverty or otherwise must be lodged with the County Treasurer on or before the 13th December, 1962. Appeals will be heard by the Finance Committee on a date to be fixed when the annual budget is presented to the Council.

ARREARS. Tenants are reminded of the need for prompt payment of charges. The County Treasurer is authorised to take immediate steps for the recovery of unpaid charges. Court action may be taken where considered appropriate for the recovery of arrears and or eviction of the tenant.

| Rent | New Rent (where changed during year) | Rateable Value | Provisional Assessment | Actual Assessment | Cooker Rental | T.V. Inst. | Stair Lighting/Garage Charges | Provisional Total Due for Year | Actual Total for Year | Provisional Amount Per Collection | Adjusted Amount Per Collection |
|---|---|---|---|---|---|---|---|---|---|---|---|
| | [illegible] | | | [illegible] | | | | | [illegible] | | 2 . 11 |

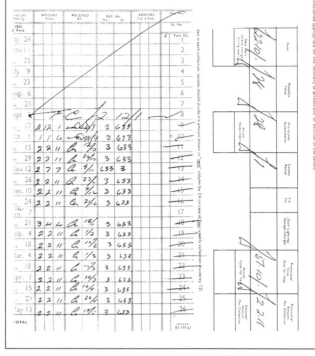

**County of Ayr — PARISH OF KILBIRNIE** FORM No. CT/E/RR/48/1

**DEMAND NOTE—RATES FOR 1959-60.**

NOTICE IS HEREBY GIVEN to the person named hereon and on the counterfoil attached hereto that the County Council of the County of Ayr acting under the Local Government (Scotland) Acts, 1889 to 1948, the Water (Scotland) Act, 1949, The Valuation and Rating (Scotland) Act, 1956, and Acts relative thereto, have levied and imposed upon such person as occupies of the lands and heritages situated as stated, County and other Rates as detailed hereon, and that for the year from 16th May, 1959 to 15th May, 1960.

1. DATE OF PAYMENT.

The rates are due and payable on or before 31st December, 1959, after which date the rates will be in arrear and liable to be recovered with the addition of Ten per cent under Summary Warrant of the Sheriff as provided by Section 247 of the Local Government (Scotland) Act, 1947.

2. REMITTANCES.

Payment may be made either to—

THE COUNTY COLLECTOR, COUNTY BUILDINGS, AYR.

or to any of the Local Collection Offices detailed in the schedule on the back hereof.
Cheques should be made payable to Ayr County Council and crossed & Co.
A stamped addressed envelope is to be sent for transmission of receipt.

3. APPEALS AND OBJECTIONS.

Any appeal against the rates, whether on the ground of poverty or otherwise, must be lodged with the County Collector on or before Monday, 14th December, 1959. Appeals will be heard and determined within the County Buildings, Ayr, on Thursday, 14th January, 1960, at 10.30 o'clock forenoon.

No appeal against the annual value appearing in the valuation roll can be entertained.

4. NOTE FOR OUTGOING OCCUPIERS.

An outgoing occupier removing during the year has a right of relief against the incoming occupier for the proportion of the Occupier's Rates applicable to the period of the year remaining unexpired at the entry of the incoming occupier.

5. OCCUPIERS RATES LEVIED ON OWNERS.

Owners are requested to notify occupiers of their right to appeal for exemption from payment of rates on the ground of poverty, etc. Such appeals must be lodged as stated in paragraph 3. Occupiers whose appeals are granted will receive an intimation to that effect. The rates involved must be paid to the County Council in the first instance by the owners and the method of repayment by the former is detailed below. In cases where no rates have been paid by occupiers, owners can recover by lodging a claim in accordance with the instructions below.

The amounts involved in exemptions to occupiers whose rates are assessed on owners in terms of Section 240 of the Local Government (Scotland) Act, 1947, will be repaid to owners on their lodging claims as stated below.

No claim in respect of occupiers rates unrecovered by owners for poverty reasons can be admitted unless accompanied by the relative intimation of exemption.

Forms for making claims by owners entitled to repayments under Section 240 of the Local Government (Scotland) Act, 1947, may be obtained on application to the County Collector.

Claims must be lodged with the County Treasurer, County Buildings, Ayr, in duplicate, between 1st and 20th May, 1960.

JOHN DALRYMPLE, *County Collector*,
COUNTY BUILDINGS, AYR.

21st November, 1959,

| VAL. FILE/ASSESSMENT No. AND DESCRIPTION | NAME | ANNUAL VALUE Gross | Rateable | Domestic Water | Code | ALL RATES EX. WATER | DOMESTIC WATER | AMOUNT PAYABLE |
|---|---|---|---|---|---|---|---|---|
| 122/24 HOUSE | [redacted] | 10. 8. 0 | 10. 10. 0 | 10. 10. 0 | 1 | 12. 5. 0 | 1. 3. 8 | 13. 8. 8 |

NAME AND AMOUNT PER £ OF RATES LEVIED

| Rates | Name | Amount per £ |
|---|---|---|
| A | COUNTY RATE (see over) | 18/5d. |
| B | KILBIRNIE DISTRICT COUNCIL RATE | 8d. |
| | SPECIAL DISTRICT RATES:- | |
| C | GARNOCK VALLEY DRAINAGE | 1/3d. |
| R | KILBIRNIE, ETC., LIGHTING AND SCAVENGING | 3/- |
| | DOMESTIC WATER RATE | 2/3d. |

| CODE | RATES | |
|---|---|---|
| 1. | ABCR | 23/4d. |
| 2. | AB | 19/1d. |
| 3. | ABC | 20/4d. |

# Monuments and Buildings

Previous chapters mention church and school buildings but there are many notable mansion houses and public buildings in Kilbirnie including the following:

*Dr Walker's Memorial, Kilbirnie*

**WALKER MEMORIAL**

Dr Walker was born in Langlands on 23rd February 1807, and was a doctor and surgeon for 52 years. He was also an ardent naturalist. He died in 1885 and the memorial originated with the Thistle Lodge of Free Gardeners of which Dr Walker was the first on the role of members and was a member for 49 years. The statue features Hygeia, the goddess of health on a pedestal on the front of which is a bronze relief of Dr Walker with a panel at the back inscribed "Wm Walker, MD born 1807, died 1885. Grateful memory of a life devoted to the wellbeing of people. The faithful physician."

*Walker Hall, Kilbirnie*

**WALKER HALL**

William Walker was the son of Dr Walker to whom the Walker Memorial was erected. He was brought up in Wallerston House on the Main Street and when he had qualified as a doctor, he emigrated to Buenos Aires where he practised medicine. In 1915 he sent a gift of £2,000 for the Kilbirnie folk; thus the Walker Hall was built—next to his old house. The Grand Opening concert took place on 9th September 1916 and the original chairman was John Riddet ex JP.

The Stables Museum is found in the old stable block of what was once a coaching inn on the main road to Glasgow which is now below the Walker Hall. This museum was created and is run by local volunteers and allows visitors a look at life in Kilbirnie over the last 150 years.

## WILLIAM KNOX INSTITUTE

It opened on Saturday 19th November 1892 and was a gift of Robert William Knox Esq of Moorpark. It was erected as a memorial to his father. The opening coincided with the 10th anniversary of the founding by his grandfather of the linen/thread business in November 1792. The architect was Mr R Snodgrass of Beith who was also the builder. The building, formerly known as the Imperial Hotel, was in later years taken over by Kilbirnie District Council and "public business" conducted there. The original hallway was laid with Minton tiles and the staircase was of bolted polished Arbroath stone with coloured glass windows. Various large rooms included a reading room, library, committee room and recreation room.

## KILBIRNIE LIBRARY

A public building but a bit "newer" than the historical ones. The library was opened in April 1975 and was the first library in Cunninghame to offer the record and music service. There have been many changes in staffing levels, book stock and the introduction of new services and the library continues to do its bit for the community. On the original site was Avil's Cottage built 1880-90 by a Mr Gollogly, whose youngest daughter inherited it but emigrated to Canada. The cottage was subsequently sold to the church and then presumably to the council. Before 1975 the library was housed in the William Knox Institute.

*Redheugh House, Kilbirnie*

## REDHEUGH

This is the oldest mansion in the parish of Kilbirnie and was built around 1840 by Hugh Knox. On his death his son moved from Knoxville to Redheugh and he was responsible for adding a substantial wing to the original house containing a new dining room, drawing room and billiard room, with bedrooms and bathrooms above. This addition was built before World War I.

> I have a photograph of myself, age three, presenting a bouquet of flowers to the then Countess of Eglinton and Winton in 1919 on the occasion of a fete in aid of the Red Cross. My grandmother lived in Redheugh and died when she was 95 leaving the house and the policies to my father who did not wish to move from Kilwinning. He had a soft spot for the Salvation Army and he disposed of it for a very small sum of money and it is now a well-known hostel for boys and girls from deprived backgrounds and broken homes and run by the Salvation Army.

*Moor Park House, Kilbirnie*

## MOORPARK

This was built by Robert William Knox in about 1848 and falls between the period of Georgian and Victorian architecture. His son was killed when serving in the army during World War I.

> My father's cousin, Annie Knox-Fletcher, lived in it until her death a few years ago. She had no children and it was inherited by three young men called Mathew who eventually disposed of it to the District Council who have restored it and use it as a Conference Room and so on.

*Place, Kilbirnie*

## PLACE

This was built by Sir James Knox, of Redheugh. Sir James built Place in about 1900 when he was Marketing Director of H & J Knox Ltd., Kilbirnie. He travelled the world, including Canada and USA moving with the two large cabin trunks, one with his personal clothing, etc., the other with boxes of Havana Cigars for his customers. He made his first Atlantic crossing in a paddle steamer in 1886 and he was required to bring his own knife, fork and spoon! He was a good salesman and brought orders and prosperity to the Mill. Sir James had two daughters, one of them was Lady Mathew, grandmother of the three boys who inherited Moorpark.

## KILBIRNIE CASTLE

This ancient building lies one mile west of the town and was the ancient seat of the Crawfurd family, the Viscounts of Garnock.

The castle was erected in two different periods. The most ancient part is an extremely high square tower, with very large walls. This is 41' long and 32' wide. The walls are 7' thick. It is also divided into 4 storeys with the lowest being vaulted. The second consisted of a hall 26' long and 18' wide, also vaulted. The hall is also lighted by a window in the south wall and another facing west. Above the hall were two tiers of chambers but now there are no traces of these. A narrow spiral stair in the north east of the building gave access to the different floors.

This tower had obviously been built for defence, however there are no gun ports. This would suggest that it was built before the invention of firearms. At the latest, the castle would have been built in the fourteenth century in the days of the Barclays which we will discover later.

The modern part of the building was built by John Crawfurd of Kilbirnie who died two years later. This was built in 1627. It is 74' long and 25' wide. It is also three storeys high and consists of attics also.

The mansion underwent repair in 1757 by George the nineteenth Earl of Crawfurd. Whilst undergoing this renovation, it was burnt to the ground by accidental fire. The carpenters had almost finished their work; they were working in the garrett storey. They did not have a fire there and for precaution, locked the doors of the apartments in the evenings when they left work. They carried the keys with them. They had left the skylight windows open however. Through these the fire found access from a foul chimney that was set on fire. One of the ladies of the family threw the melted grease from the candle socket into a grate in the lower storey, just as she was going to bed.

*Kilbirnie Castle*

The true cause was only divulged 24 years later when the Earl died.

The building is now in a state of collapse and little remains of the walled orchards and pleasure grounds.

## FIRE AT KILBIRNIE CASTLE

The fire at Kilbirnie Castle on 1st May 1757 occurred in the early morning and spread with such rapidity that the Earl just had time to save his infant daughter, Jean (afterwards Countess of Eglinton) and with his family and servants he rushed from the house. It was never re-occupied. One version has it that the fire was started by one of the ladies of the family throwing the melted grease from the socket of a candlestick into the grate. According to Dobie in 1880, "it is known" that the fire was started by sparks from one of the chimney tops falling into the garret through an open window.

The Earl died in 1781 and was succeeded by his son George, the 70th Earl. On George's death, in 1808, Kilbirnie and the other estates in Ayrshire, Dumbartonshire and Fifeshire passed to his sister, Lady Mary Lindsay Crawfurd, who held them untill her death in 1833, when George, 4th Earl of Glasgow, succeeded her in virtue of his descent from Margaret, oldest daughter of Patrick Lindsay and Margaret Crawfurd, who had married David, 1st Earl of Glasgow. They descended to the present Earl of Glasgow and remained in his possession till the breaking up of his estates, when the old fortress of the Crawfurds passed by purchase into the hands of Sir James Knox.

## GLENGARNOCK

The Estate of Glengarnock anciently belonged to a branch of the family of Ridel.

Gervas Ridel was a witness to the Inquisitio Davidis, in 1116, and was a frequent witness to the Charters of that Prince after he ascended to the throne. Other members of the family rose to distinction and acquired considerable landed estates in various districts of Scotland.

One branch early on acquired the Estate of Glengarnock. Prior to 1268, Ridel the Heiress of Glengarnock, was married to Harvey Cunninghame, the Heir of Kilmaurs, who distinguished himself at the Battle of Largs.

Galfridus Cunninghame, the 2nd son of this marriage, was the ancestor of the Cunninghames of Glengarnock who held the Estate for several centuries. Umfridus Cunninghame of Glengarnock sat in Parliament in Edinburgh, 2nd April 1481 in the reign of James III. His daughter Agnes was married to Sir Andrew Moray of Abercairney and their son John married Agnes, daughter of the Master of Montgomery.

The family of Glengarnock continued for several centuries but latterly fell, and the Estate was acquired by the family of Kilbirnie.

The Manor place of Glengarnock Estate was Glengarnock Castle.

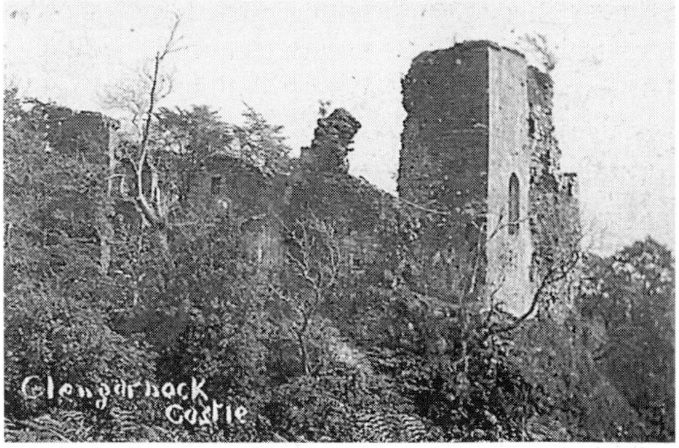


*Glengarnock Castle*

## GLENGARNOCK CASTLE

This castle is one of the most ancient ruins in Ayrshire. It stands on top of a very high rock about two miles north of town.

The rock on which it stands appears to be around one hundred feet in height.

There are features which indicate there was a dry moat there with a drawbridge.

The castle itself consisted of a quadrilateral tower in a court of smaller buildings which extended from the east side. The facade was 46' long and 24' high. A passage which was 59' long lay between the entrance and tower. On each side there lay a range of two storey apartments.

The tower itself was 45' long and 33' wide and 40' in height. A circular stair led to the upper floors.

Like Kilbirnie Castle, there are no gun ports. Perhaps natural defences proved these unnecessary.

There is no account of when this was erected or by whom but it may have been erected by its last Lords the Cunninghame family or by the Ridels who preceded them.

Some say that Glengarnock Castle was the ancient castle of Hardyknute which is just as well known as a famous battle, the Battle of Largs.

The north wall of the castle was destroyed in January of 1839 by storms.

## OLD TOLL HOUSE

The Old Toll House was one of three Toll Houses—the picture shows the Toll House which was next to the Barony. The other two were—one at Stoneyholm Road and one on the Largs Road at the turning to Dalry. This latter features in a Robert Houston painting. These Toll Houses were installed to help finance the turn pike roads which local people also had to finance.

*Old Toll-House*
*Auld Kirk in the background*

## THE BARONY

The Barony was the original manse of the Auld Kirk and it is thought the house was built in 1769 with outbuildings added later. There is a date stone on one of them saying 1796. The Rev Buchan moved to the Manse in 1886 and though the house had been inspected prior to this, he decided a lot of work was required including the installation of a bathroom. All the work, for example rebuilding of the front porch, redecoration inside and out, floor repairs etc. was agreed to for the sum of £30 but there was a negative vote on the provision of a bathroom. It was 1898 before the Rev Buchan finally got his bathroom and the stories go that he actually died in that room. The Barony is still occupied but is no longer the church manse.

*Avinhaugh*

## AVINHAUGH

Avinhaugh was built between 1871 and 1881 for the Watt family who owned the rope works. They originally lived in Waterside Cottage but as the firm and their prosperity grew, they could afford the upkeep of larger accommodation. In 1907 the house was split into four flats and some of the family continued to live there, latterly in one of the flats. John Watt and Sons went into voluntary liquidation and the flat was held in trust by the Earl of Glasgow for John Watt and was transferred to the Watt sisters in 1936. They owned the flat until 1957 when it was sold to Sarah and Jeanne Thomson. Sarah died in 1973 but Jeanne stayed in the flat untill 1988. Avinhaugh is still occupied as four separate flats today, in 1995, and is situated in Milton Road, Kilbirnie.

## CO-OP BUILDINGS, GLENGARNOCK

The original building housed a number of shops—grocer, shoe, cobbler, dairy and butchers—with flats above. The building still stands with the bottom being occupied by the Jehovahs Witness Hall and some flats above. The original clock is still on the corner—apparently in years gone by, the rent of the flat housing the clock was cheaper—in return the tenants wound the clock!

## LADYLAND

The barony of Ladyland belonged for centuries to a cadet of the Barclays of Kilbirnie but was sold in 1669 to Captain William Hamilton from whose family it passed prior to 1710. Soon after it was purchased by Alexander 9th Earl of Eglinton who in 1718 feued it to William Cochran of Edge.

The old house in 1608, characterised by Pont as a "Stronge Touer" was almost completely demolished in 1815. There was a cavity in one of the walls just above the foundations which was found to contain a few small urns, a painted drinking glass and a large saw bone. Three of the urns contained "unctuous earth" the fourth also containing the breast and side bones of a chicken. They were all tightly closed and are still preserved at Ladyland along with a small metal coin. William Cochran rebuilt Ladyland in 18th July 1918 on the site of the Strong Tower. It passed through generations of the Cochran family and was finally sold, but is still a family home today.

*Ladyland*

*War Memorial*

## WAR MEMORIAL

The war memorial was unveiled on 8th October 1922. It was a unique ceremony in that as well as showing reverence to the war dead, it had a practical use for the living, being also the gateway to the new public park. The archway is neo Greek style and was designed by Mr James Houston. Bronze tablets on each side of the gateway contain the names of 159 men who sacrificed their lives. The park that the gateway leads to extends to about 17 acres and a few thousand people turned up for the opening ceremony of unveiling the memorial and opening the park. The unveiling was performed by Major General Sir Charles M Matthew KCMG CB DSS and was preceded by a procession through the town of ex servicemen, guides, brethren of the Masonic Lodge, school children, Good Templers and members of the friendly societies accompanied by many bands. Mr John Riddet JP and chairman of the parish council then formally declared the park open. The park is well used by residents and has swings, playpark area, putting green, tennis courts and football pitches and the swimming pool is also on site there.

## SCULPTURE, KILBIRNIE CROSS

The sculpture was erected on 8th June 1974 and the sculptor was John Henry White ARBS who had a studio at Howwood in Renfrewshire. It is made of sheet metal from Gartcosh and had to be cleaned

*Sculpture, Kilbirnie Cross*

in 1986 as steel proved to be corrosive. The sculpture was unveiled by Andrew Young the then chairman of Scottish Division of British Steel. Previously, the Kilbirnie Christmas tree was put at the cross.

## CRAWFURD MAUSOLEUM

Erected in 1594 by Captain Thomas Crawfurd of Jordanhill for himself and his lady. It stands out of the church and is $9^{1}/_{2}$' long and 6' wide and $6^{1}/_{2}$' high. It is decorated with Gothic Ornaments. There is an aperture at the east end of the monument through which can be seen the recumbent statues of the gallant captain in military garb and of his spouse in the costume of the time. The hands of the back figure are joined in the breast as in prayer. Captain Crâwfurd died and was buried alongside the inscribed wall of the monument on 30 January 1603 as is still indicated by a flat stone bearing his name. The motto on the monument "God Shaw the richt" was conferred on Captain Crawfurd by the Earl of Morton in 1571.

*Crawfurd Mausoleum*

## JUBILEE BUILDING

This was built in 1894 to celebrate Queen Victoria's Jubilee—the Co-op store was in the corner later occupied by Hunter the baker. The building was demolished in 1992.

*Jubilee Building*

## KILBIRNIE FARMS

Kilbirnie and Glengarnock are still very much home to a large farming community and many of the original farms are still lived in although they may not be working farms.

From the electoral register in 1995, we list the following farms and there are roads in Kilbirnie named after some of them:

*Causewayfoot Farm*

Birtlebog, Blackburn, Cockstone, East Bankside, Geirston, Greeridge, High Glengarth, Birtlehill, Holehouse, Bashaw, Ainville, Kaimhill, Laigh Auchengree, Little Auchengree, Meikle Auchengree, Laigh Glengarth, Glenlodge, North Dykes, Plan, North Hourat, Elnside, Rashleyelt, Wallace, Wattieston, West Bankside, Whiteridden, East Lochridge, Lochside and Baillieston where there once was an illicit whisky still!

Obviously farming has changed very much over the years with access to modern farming methods and machinery. Sunday schools and guides often "borrowed" a field to have picnics or camp for the night. Farmers still rise very early and go to bed late, particularly dairy farmers and the various types of farms form a close knit community. We have beef farms, cropping farms, sheep farms and farms are passed down from generation to generation. Usually the eldest son inherits the parents farm and the parents' move to a house on the land. The Young Farmers arrange various community events from dances to concerts which are enjoyed by the whole community. The Beith District Young Farmers (of which Kilbirnie and Glengarnock are part) now hold their shows in the Magnum in Irvine—a big venue which is well attended.

At Holehouse Farm, the records show that the Logan and Fife family paid rent as far back as 1725. At that time there was East and West Holehouse farms. The Logans left Holehouse and stayed on in the area but its not known where. The Fifes continued to farm, amalgamating East and West Holehouse untill 1912 when the Logans returned.

The present Mrs Logan Snr is a direct descendant of the Fife family and married into the Logan family in 1944.

## THE LAMP AT KILBIRNIE CROSS

The lamp at Kilbirnie Cross was erected in 1904 by way of thanks to RW Knox—the major employers in the town. It was placed in the wall at the side of the burn across from Knox's Institute but was moved in 1927 when the Cross was altered and the bridge moved. The original gas lamp was placed at the roundabout but was replaced by an electric one in the 1930s. The stone can be found in the Stables Museum (under the Walker Hill). The lamp was placed at the side of the Institute but later fell apart and was removed.

*The Lamp at Kilbirnie Cross*

# Retrospective

Kilbirnie and Glengarnock have had their fair share of documented events which have been mentioned throughout our account. There are a few which we feel we must expand on giving greater detail:

## CRANNOGS AND CANOES

Crannogs or "artificial islands", built of brushwood or stone in lochs or estuaries, were very common throughout Scotland and in 1868 evidence of these were discovered in Kilbirnie Loch.

The weight of the Slag Hill at the side of Kilbirnie Loch forced the level of mud at the bottom of the loch to rise and bring into view evidence of a crannog and also the remains of a canoe or boat.

One of these canoes, found in 1868, contained a lion shaped ewer and a three-legged pot of bronze.

It is described as being hollowed out of a single tree and about 18' in length, 3' broad and approximately 2' deep.

The lion stands 8$^1/_2$ high and weighs around 4lbs. It is made of yellowish bronze and seemed to have been used to hold some form of liquid.

The bronze pot stood approximately 14" high by 11" wide and weighed around 28lbs. It resembled what was often called a Roman Camp Kettle.

The items found in the canoe are apparently from a different period than the canoe itself and there is some doubt as to why they were found together.

A further canoe was discovered in roughly the same area in 1930 giving further evidence of inhabitation on the loch itself.

*The Ancient Dug-out Canoe photographed at Kelvingrove Museum.* **Daily Record** *Photo.*

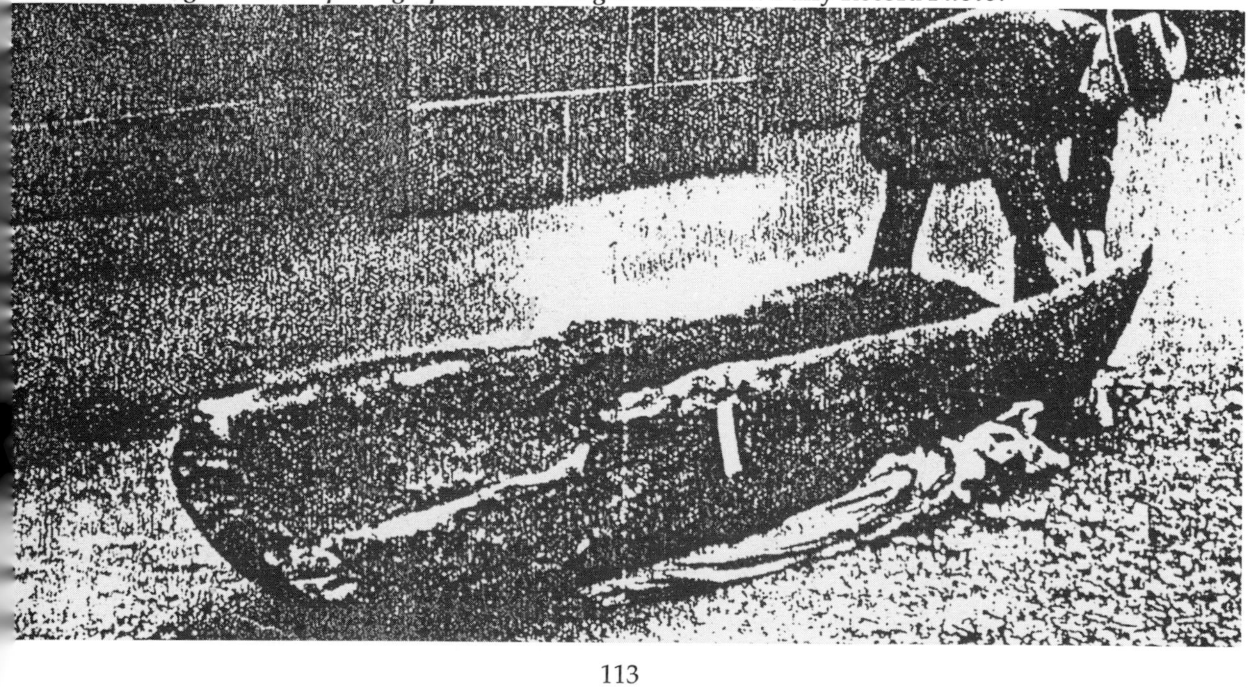

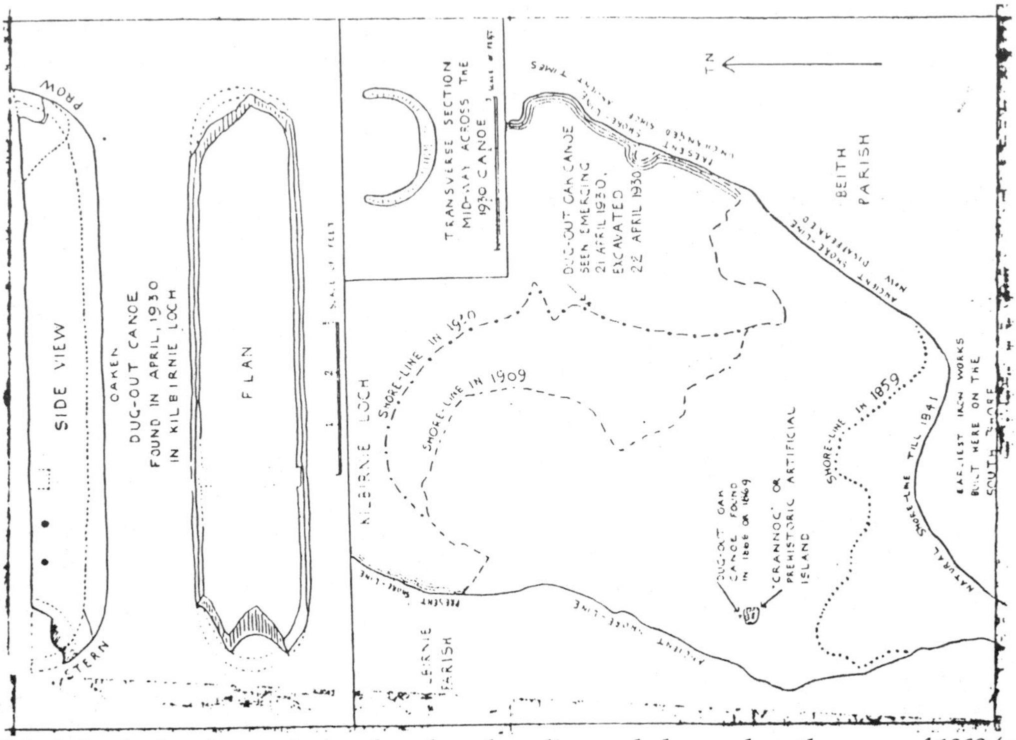


*Plan of Kilbirnie Loch, showing ancient and modern shore-line, and places where the canoe of 1868 (and crannog) and the canoe of 1930 was discovered. Superimposed are scale drawings of the recently found vessel.*

## FLOODS

20th August 1910 is a date that will be remembered as the big flood in Kilbirnie. The waters of the River Garnock rose to such an extent that it reached the bottom of Cochrane Street and in the process washed away the Mill Road and people could only stand by and watch.

*Kilbirnie Flood 1910*

The torrential rain that fell in August 1956 once again caused the Garnock to flood, causing great damage to property because the normal precautions had not been taken, as this type of weather was unusual for the time of the year!

*View from the Station in Glengarnock. August 1956*

The river was cleaned and deepened after the last flood in September 1978, but it still floods, the latest being the end of 1994 when residents had to leave their homes, many of which were badly damaged.

## WAR

Memories of war: departures, homecomings, Home Guard, rationing, war brides, camaraderie, lives sacrificed, changes of occupation are known to all and many pictures are indelibly engraved in peoples' minds.

*1st World War*

*Home Guard*

## SERVICES

Services are provided in many areas of our lives and can go unnoticed, but on occasion a presentation of thanks is made to show gratitude to those who have cared for the people of Kilbirnie and Glengarnock for many years of their lives.

***James Duffield (Snr), on left, receives Long Service Recognition medal.***

*Fire Service*

# Events

*Lady Cochran Patrick's Tenants Day Out. (Early 1900s)*

*Dr Begg (Snr) – fith from left – Retiral.*

*Dr Begg (Jnr) Retiral*

# Kilbirnie Fire Station

## Dedication Service

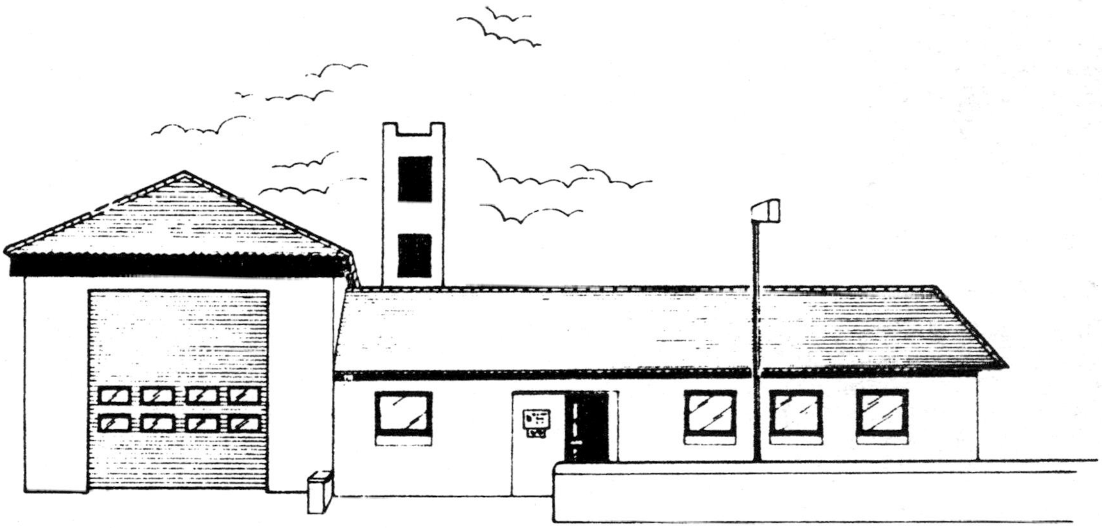

*Tuesday 19th December 1989*
*1900 hours*

JUNE 2ND 1953
THE
ROYAL DAY

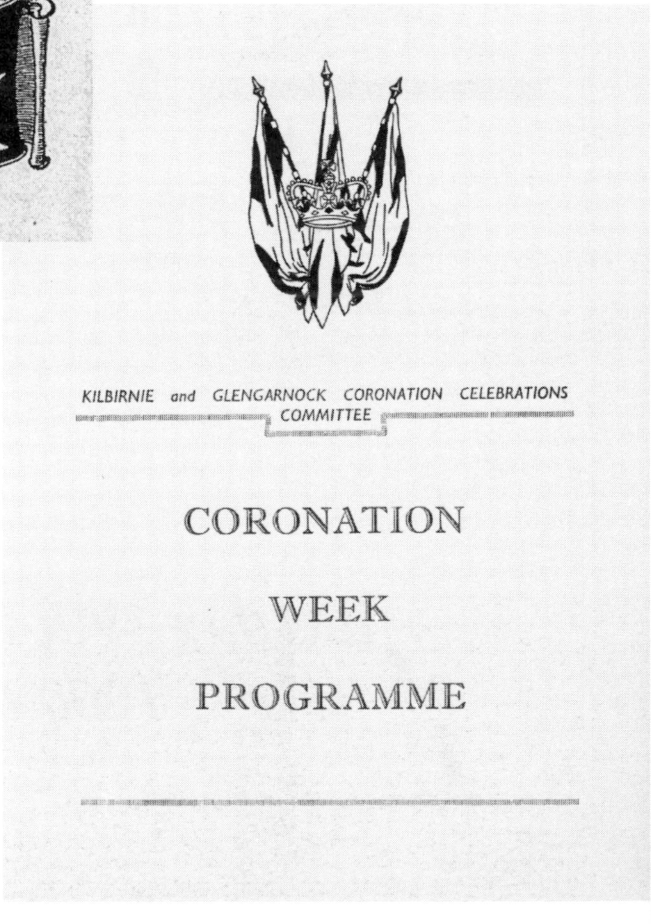
KILBIRNIE and GLENGARNOCK CORONATION CELEBRATIONS
COMMITTEE
CORONATION
WEEK
PROGRAMME

★ ★
★

# "CORONATION 1953."

★ ★ ★

*Monday, 1st June.*

7.30 p.m. Service of Praise in the Public Park.

8.30 p.m. Service of Intercession in the Old Parish Church.

★ ★ ★

*Tuesday, 2nd June.*

## "CORONATION DAY"

2.30 till 5 p.m. Games for school children under the direction of the Children's Committee in Valefield. Distribution of Ices, Presentation of Prizes, etc.

*Musical Recitals by KILBIRNIE CITADEL BAND in Kilbirnie and Glengarnock.*

6 p.m. FANCY DRESS PARADE.

1. Fancy Dress Rider and Cycle.
2. Fancy Dress Pedestrian. *(Age groups, 5-8, 9-12, 13 and over)*
3. Decorated Vehicles. or Tableaux entered by local schools.
4. Decorated Commercial Motor Vehicles, Cars, Tractors, etc.
5. Horses, Horse Drawn Vehicles, Ponies, etc.
6. Most Original Turnout.

Muster at Muirend Street, then proceed to Public Park for judging by the Committee in respect of the various sections. Presentation of Prizes. *(KILBIRNIE and DISTRICT PIPE BAND will lead)*

PUBLIC PARK.

7.30 p.m. DANCING DISPLAY. By Pupils of Seestu School of Dancing. *(Miss Nancy Dickson).*

8-11 p.m. OPEN AIR DANCING. *Music by GRAHAM'S BAND.*

10.30 p.m. BONFIRE and FIREWORKS DISPLAY.

*TEAS will be served in the Public Park from 7 p.m. onwards.*

★ ★ ★

WALKER MEMORIAL HALL.

*Wednesday, 3rd June.*

## OLD FOLK'S CONCERT.

7.30 p.m. ARTISTES

Alex Carmichael *Bass Baritone.*
Janette Sclanders *Soprano.*
George McCormack *Tenor.*
Nan Scott *Elocutionist.*
Garnock Choral Society.

★ ★ ★

*Thursday, 4th June.*

7.30 p.m. TEENAGER'S DANCE.

★ ★ ★

*Friday, 4th June.*

8 p.m. CORONATION BALL.

★ ★ ★

### *St. Brinius's Day*

# KILBIRNIE and GLENGARNOCK : : : : DISTRICT NURSING and AMBULANCE ASSOCIATION

## Opening Ceremony

: : at NEW CLINIC : :

Saturday, 11th April, 1931, at 3 p.m.

**Honorary Presidents:**
Captain DAVID COLVILLE. Major JOHN COLVILLE, M.P.
Mr. G. P. WEST. Mr. JAMES KNOX. Mrs. JAMES KNOX.
Mrs. N. J. K. COCHRAN-PATRICK. Mrs. BRYCE M. KNOX.

**President:**
Mr. P. A. ABERNETHY.

**Vice-Presidents:**
Mr. JAMES DAVIDSON. Mr. HENRY MCTAGGART.

**Hon. Treasurer:**
Mr. ALEXANDER BRUCE, J.P.

**Convenor of Property Committee:**
Mr. THOMAS CLARK.

**Assistant Secretary (Ambulance Section):**
Mr. ALEX. MCCALLUM.

**Assistant Secretary (Nursing Section):**
Mrs. D. G. ROBERTSON.

**General Secretary:**
Mr. ROBERT MCWHINNIE.

**Nurses:**
Miss ROBERTA COOPER. Miss JANET B. STEWART.

**Ambulance Car Driver:**
Mr. DAVID AITKEN.

**Auditors:**
Mr. JOHN DRYSDALE. Mr FRANCIS MCDONALD, J.P.

**Executive Committee:**

| | |
|---|---|
| Mrs. R. Ferguson. | Mrs. D. G. Robertson. |
| Mr. Peter A. Abernethy | Mr. James Davidson. |
| ,, Henry McTaggart. | ,, Alex. McCallum. |
| ,, Thomas Clark. | ,, John P. Sharp. |
| ,, Alex. Bruce, J.P. | ,, Robert McWhinnie |

**General Committee:**

| | |
|---|---|
| Mrs. Bell. | Mr. William Shaw. |
| ,, Fraser. | ,, James Shaw. |
| ,, McNeil. | ,, John Dick. |
| ,, McCulloch. | ,, Hugh Wallace. |
| ,, McLennan. | ,, Robert Fyfe. |
| ,, Bray. | ,, Francis McDonald, J.P. |
| ,, Brown. | ,, Robert Anderson. |
| ,, McGrath. | ,, Wm. H. Frame. |
| ,, John Knox. | ,, Robert Dick. |
| ,, Reynolds. | ,, Hugh Munro, C.C., J.P. |
| ,, Carlyle. | ,, John Barclay. |
| ,, McCulloch. | ,, William Purdie. |
| Mr. John Riddet, J.P. | ,, Michael Curran. |
| ,, Robert Craig, C.C. | ,, James Gibson. |
| ,, George L. Whitelaw. | ,, Daniel McGrath. |
| ,, Patrick Loy. | ,, Robert Ferguson. |
| ,, John McGrath. | ,, John Knox. |
| ,, David Houston. | ,, John McBlane. |
| ,, Wm. Lang. | ,, James Berry. |
| ,, Wm. Bryson. | ,, Thomas Graham. |

Mr. George Dickie.

COMMERCIAL HOTEL
(Mrs. I. Walker)
Seven Day License
LUNCHES SERVED FROM 12.30 P.M.
BED AND BREAKFAST 6/6
MAIN STREET
KILBIRNIE

ROBERT HENDERSON
Joiner and Funeral Undertaker
*Personal attention to all work*
ESTIMATES GIVEN FREE
DISTANCE NO OBJECT
SCHOOL WYND - KILBIRNIE
House Address – 18 Munro Drive

HUGH LAW
General Ironmonger
Ironmongery in all its branches
Enquiries invited
87 MAIN STREET
KILBIRNIE

When in Beith or Kilbirnie

GARAGE
at
WALKER'S
Telephones
Beith 73. Kilbirnie—Beith 140

PETROL, OILS, ACCESSORIES
and prompt and courteous attention to your requirements at all times

Motor Accessories
Hearse, Buses and Cars for Hire
Repairs and Overhauls
Wireless Sets and Accessories stocked
Hercules and Rudge-Whitworth Cycles

BEST QUALITY
BUTCHER MEAT
GUARANTEED
PRIME HOME FED

ROBERT HARKNESS
*Butcher & Poulterer*
85 MAIN STREET
KILBIRNIE

DAY AND NIGHT SERVICE
ARCHIBALD LENNOX
Funeral Undertaker
Hearse and Motor Hirer
THE GARAGE, COCHRANE STREET
also 81 MAIN STREET
KILBIRNIE
Phone - Beith 95
BRANCH – MITCHELL STREET, BEITH
Phone - Beith 148

*Strathclyde Regional Council Convener Jimmy Jennings and Deputy-Firemaster John Jamieson were among some of the invited guests at the special Dedication Service at Kilbirnie Fire Station*

*Centenary ceilidh, February 1970*

## AN OPEN BOOK?

We could not end the book without leaving an opening for a "sequel". Do you know the answers?—If you do, let us know!

### FLASHBACK TO OLD KILBIRNIE

The year is early this century—before the First World War. The place—Kilbirnie. A procession comes along Bridge Street approaching Kilbirnie Cross.

This picture which appeared in one of our editions some years ago, caused some controversy as to the actual date it was taken and what was the occasion of the street procession. In fact, neither question was satisfactorily answered at the time.

Since then our sales in the Garnock area have increased enormously and with the much larger readership of today we are throwing open the question again. Who were the band who brought out the enthusiastic onlookers, and when was this picture taken? The Editor will be glad to have any information from readers.

*From Ardrossan & Saltcoats Herald*

WORLD BELIEFS AND CULTURES

# Hinduism

*Revised and updated*

Sue Penney

Heinemann
LIBRARY

www.heinemann.co.uk/library
Visit our website to find out more information about Heinemann Library books.

To order:
Phone 44 (0) 1865 888066
Send a fax to 44 (0) 1865 314091
Visit the Heinemann Bookshop at www.heinemann.co.uk/library to browse our catalogue and order online.

First published in Great Britain by Heinemann Library, Halley Court, Jordan Hill, Oxford OX2 8EJ, part of Pearson Education. Heinemann is a registered trademark of Pearson Education Ltd.



Editorial: Nancy Dickmann
Design: Steve Mead and Debbie Oatley
Picture research: Melissa Allison
Production: Alison Parsons

Originated by Modern Age Repro
Printed and bound in China by Leo Paper Group

13 digit ISBN: 978 0 431 11030 1 (HB)
12 11 10 09 08
10 9 8 7 6 5 4 3 2 1

13 digit ISBN: 978 0 431 11037 0 (PB)
13 12 11 10 09
10 9 8 7 6 5 4 3 2 1

**British Library Cataloguing in Publication Data**
Penney, Sue
Hinduism. – (World Beliefs and Cultures)
1. Hinduism – Juvenile literature
I. Title
294.5
A full catalogue record for this book is available from the British Library.

**Acknowledgements**
The publishers would like to thank the following for permission to reproduce photographs: Andes Press Agency/Carlos Reyes-Manzo pp. **5**, **10**, **16**, **22**, **29**, **30**, **35**, **38**; Ann and Bury Peerless pp. **7**, **12**, **17**, **20**, **37**, **43**; Art Directors/Helene Rogers pp. **18**, **34**; Christine Osborne Pictures pp. **6**, **8**, **9**, **21**, **23**, **26**, **36**, **40**, **41**; Circa Photos Library pp. **11** (John Smith), **14** (Bipin J. Mistry), **25** (William Holtby), **32** (Robyn Beeche); Corbis pp. p. **39** (Bob Krist), **42** (James Leynse); Corbis/Reuters/Ajay Verma, p. **28**; FLPA/E. and D. Hosking, p. **4**; Hutchison pp. **24**, **27**, **31**, **33**; Mary Evans Picture Library p. **13**. Background image on cover and inside book from istockphoto.com/ Bart Broek.

Cover photo of a Hindu deity reproduced with permission of © Getty Images/Taxi.

Our thanks to Philip Emmett for his comments in the preparation of this book.